Teaching mental strategies

number calculations in Years 5 and 6

by Mike Askew, Debbie Robinson and Fran Mosley

BEAM Education

our thanks to

teachers from Islington, Camden
and Brent for their incisive comment
and continuing support

Published by BEAM Education
© BEAM Education 2001
All rights reserved
ISBN 1 903142 20 2

Designed and typeset by BEAM Education

Printed in England by Beshara Press

British Library Cataloguing-in-Publication
Data

A catalogue record for this publication is
available from the British Library

other books in the series
Teaching mental strategies
number calculations in Years 1 and 2
ISBN 1 903142 18 0

Teaching mental strategies
number calculations in Years 3 and 4
ISBN 1 903142 19 9

Foreword

The temptation to just 'teach the objectives', when you get to the main part of the mathematics lesson – and you are trying to implement the National Numeracy Strategy – can be very strong. Teachers who adopt this 'transmission' approach may go through the work that has to be covered addressing only very specific, closed questions to children, and then follow this by giving all children a set of similar exercises to work through on their own. This approach, while useful on occasion, leaves little space for children to develop and explain their own ideas and strategies, either to the class or to other children while working in pairs or groups. Children may start to get the message that in mathematics they only have to remember, and not to think – and they will then find it difficult to select strategies to apply in new situations.

This new series of books from BEAM will help teachers both address the objectives and challenge children to think, to come up with strategies and to discuss and share their ideas with others. *Teaching mental strategies* will help teachers anticipate what strategies may be suggested or which ones to introduce if no one spontaneously comes up with them. The series therefore addresses the true intentions of the Numeracy Strategy: by encouraging genuinely interactive lessons.

I am sure that teachers will find these books enormously helpful, and I wholeheartedly recommend them.

Professor Margaret Brown

School of Education
King's College London

contents

Salwa.M

contents

Introduction

how to teach mental strategies?

an alternative approach

We know that numerate pupils have a broad range of mental strategies to draw on when calculating. So mental strategies are learnable, but what is the best way to teach them? One approach is to itemise as many of the strategies as possible, choose an order to teach them in, work through this list and then apply the strategies. This is a bit like the way that manuals for word-processing packages work.

But anyone who has learnt to word process knows that working through a manual can be quite frustrating. The order in which manuals are put together represents the writer's perception of what is needed, rather than the user's, and these do not always coincide. It is no use being taught about font sizes if what you want to learn is how to cut and paste. Similarly, working through a series of mental strategies may not reflect the order in which the learner needs to encounter them.

An alternative approach to teaching strategies and then applying them is to start with a problem-solving situation and see what strategies are needed. This approach means drawing on the cyclical relationship between learning a strategy and using it. Being presented with a problem to solve may make you realise that your existing strategies are not adequate and provoke you into seeking out new ones. As your knowledge of strategies expands, so you can tackle more problems.

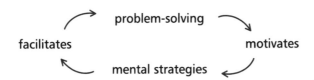

This book provides both problem-solving challenges and ideas for teaching strategies, so that the above cycle can be entered at any point. By starting from a problem-solving situation, pupils can come to appreciate the need for effective strategies and so be motivated to learn them.

how to use this book

Teaching mental strategies presents twenty-four challenges for you to work on with your pupils. Each challenge has been designed to engage children's interest in the mathematics whilst requiring them to use mental strategies appropriate to their age and level of attainment. All the challenges in this book contain material that can be used with children in both Year 5 and Year 6. It is up to you how and when you choose to introduce, for example, challenges using decimal notation; this will depend on your knowledge of the needs and abilities of the children in the class you are teaching. Equally, some of the challenges will be consolidation activities for Year 6 children, some of whom may need more opportunities for revision and reinforcement than others.

We recommend that you set the children off on the challenge and give them time to get involved before attending to the strategies that they use.

Each challenge is set out over a double-page spread. A detailed account of how each spread works is given on page 9.

how to teach mental strategies?

when to teach the strategies

There are several ways that you can introduce new strategies as the children work on the challenges. Firstly, through your observations of the children as they work on the strategies, you might decide that it is appropriate to intervene and demonstrate an alternative strategy there and then. Even if children are not using the most efficient or effective strategy, it is best to let them carry on using it for a little while, so that they appreciate that there may be a better way to work things out.

Secondly, you may decide to stop everyone from working on the challenge before they reach a conclusion and discuss the various strategies being used. Children can explain their different methods and the class can discuss the merits of each. To get the most out of such a discussion it is better to select in advance who you are going to ask to explain to the class, rather than simply ask for volunteers. That way you can ensure you get a range of strategies and, over time, ensure that different children have the opportunity to report back.

To assist you in keeping track of the different strategies that children use, a photocopiable chart of all the strategies is provided on page 63.

Sometimes, you may decide that it is better to let the children work until they resolve the challenge, and then look at the different strategies in the plenary sessions. Once the children have developed a range of strategies you may occasionally decide to go over one or two of the strategies before the children start on the challenge, to remind them about methods.

Using your professional judgement and knowledge of the particular children in your class means you can teach the strategies at different times, so that a balance can be maintained between letting the children use their own methods and moving them on to something more efficient when the time seems right.

learning styles

Many of the mental strategies are needed for more than one challenge. Where this is the case, different styles of teaching the strategies are introduced: some visual, some more oral, some practical. In this way, children's different learning styles can be catered for, and when an individual has difficulty appreciating a strategy presented in one way, you can find a possible alternative. The learning grid at the front of each section will help you see where else the strategies are discussed.

formative assessment

The challenges can also be used as tools for formative assessment. Setting the children off on a challenge and then observing a group of children will provide insight into the thinking of the children. The chart on page 63 provides a record-keeping device for this.

how to teach mental strategies?

This page describes the mental strategies that you can teach (or revise) at any point during the challenge.

This page sets out the challenge as a step-by-step classroom activity.

This tells you at a glance which calculation the children will practise.

This is a brief description of the challenge.

This is the equipment you will need.

Each strategy is described in detail, with examples.

Here are the mental strategies that accompany this challenge.

Each challenge is numbered

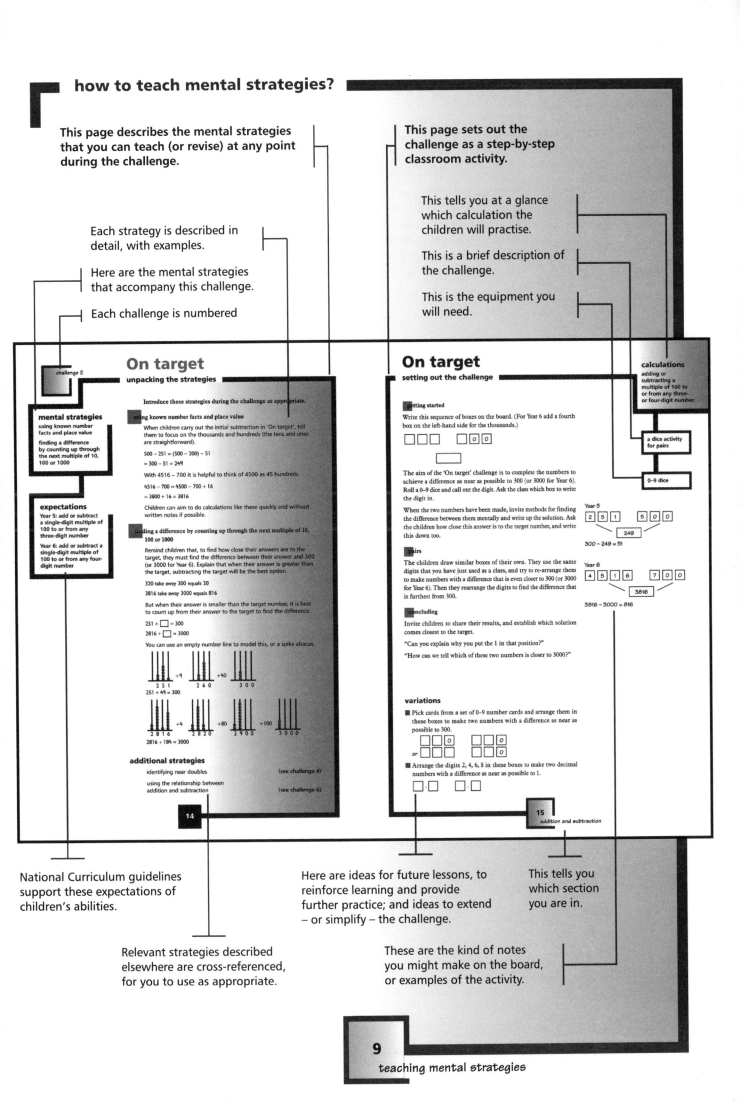

On target
unpacking the strategies

challenge 2

Introduce these strategies during the challenge as appropriate.

mental strategies
using known number facts and place value

finding a difference by counting up through the next multiple of 10, 100 or 1000

expectations
Year 5: add or subtract a single-digit multiple of 100 to or from any three-digit number

Year 6: add or subtract a single-digit multiple of 100 to or from any four-digit number

using known number facts and place value

When children carry out the initial subtraction in 'On target', tell them to focus on the thousands and hundreds (the tens and ones are straightforward).

500 − 251 = (500 − 200) − 51
= 300 − 51 = 249

With 4516 − 700 it is helpful to think of 4500 as 45 hundreds.

4516 − 700 = 4500 − 700 + 16
= 3800 + 16 = 3816

Children can aim to do calculations like these quickly and without written notes if possible.

finding a difference by counting up through the next multiple of 10, 100 or 1000

Remind children that, to find how close their answers are to the target, they must find the difference between their answer and 300 (or 3000 for Year 6). Explain that when their answer is greater than the target, subtracting the target will be the best option.

320 take away 300 equals 20

3816 take away 3000 equals 816

But when their answer is smaller than the target number, it is best to count up from their answer to the target to find the difference.

251 + □ = 300
2816 + □ = 3000

You can use an empty number line to model this, or a spike abacus.

251 +9 260 +40 300
251 + 49 = 300

2816 +4 2820 +80 2900 +100 3000
2816 + 184 = 3000

additional strategies

identifying near doubles (see challenge 4)

using the relationship between addition and subtraction (see challenge 6)

14

On target
setting out the challenge

calculations
adding or subtracting a multiple of 100 to or from any three- or four-digit number

a dice activity for pairs

0–9 dice

getting started

Write this sequence of boxes on the board. (For Year 6 add a fourth box on the left-hand side for the thousands.)

□□□ □0 0

The aim of the 'On target' challenge is to complete the numbers to achieve a difference as near as possible to 300 (or 3000 for Year 6). Roll a 0–9 dice and call out the digit. Ask the class which box to write the digit in.

When the two numbers have been made, invite methods for finding the difference between them mentally and write up the solution. Ask the children how close this answer is to the target number, and write this down too.

pairs

The children draw similar boxes of their own. They use the same digits that you have just used as a class, and try to re-arrange them to make numbers with a difference that is even closer to 300 (or 3000 for Year 6). Then they rearrange the digits to find the difference that is furthest from 300.

concluding

Invite children to share their results, and establish which solution comes closest to the target.

"Can you explain why you put the 1 in that position?"

"How can we tell which of these two numbers is closer to 3000?"

Year 5
2 5 1   5 0 0
249
300 − 249 = 51

Year 6
4 5 1 6   7 0 0
3816
3816 − 3000 = 816

variations

■ Pick cards from a set of 0–9 number cards and arrange them in these boxes to make two numbers with a difference as near as possible to 300.

□□□ 0   □□□ 0
or □□□ 0   □□□ 0

■ Arrange the digits 2, 4, 6, 8 in these boxes to make two decimal numbers with a difference as near as possible to 1.

□·□   □·□

15
addition and subtraction

National Curriculum guidelines support these expectations of children's abilities.

Here are ideas for future lessons, to reinforce learning and provide further practice; and ideas to extend – or simplify – the challenge.

This tells you which section you are in.

Relevant strategies described elsewhere are cross-referenced, for you to use as appropriate.

These are the kind of notes you might make on the board, or examples of the activity.

Addition
and subtraction

a set of eight challenges

10

the learning grid

calculations	1 Two by three	2 On target	3 Ask the audience	4 The golden triangle	5 Go digital	6 Mix and match	7 As luck would have it	8 The diamond run
adding or subtracting three-digit numbers	■							
adding or subtracting a multiple of 100 to or from any three- or four-digit number		■						
adding or subtracting pairs of multiples of 10			■					
adding several numbers				■				
adding or subtracting a pair of decimal numbers					■			
adding three or more three-digit multiples of 100						■		
finding what to add to a decimal number to make the next higher whole number							■	
finding the difference between a pair of numbers lying either side of a multiple of 1000								■

strategies	1	2	3	4	5	6	7	8
finding a small difference by counting up					■		■	
finding a difference by counting up through the next multiple of 10, 100 or 1000	□	■				■		■
partitioning into hundreds, tens and ones	■			□		□		
partitioning into thousands, hundreds and tens			■					
identifying near doubles		□	□	■				
adding or subtracting a near multiple of 10, and adjusting			■			■		
adding or subtracting a near multiple of 100 (or 1000), and adjusting	■							
subtracting a near multiple of 10, 100 or 1000, and adjusting								■
using the relationship betweeen addition and subtraction	□	□			□	■	□	□
looking for pairs that make 10 or a multiple of 10				■				
putting the larger number first	■		□				□	
using known number facts and place value		■			□		■	□
using the relationship between multiplication and addition				■				
using partitioning to add or subtract pairs of decimal numbers							■	

■ this strategy is described in detail here
□ this strategy is referred to as an additional option here

Two by three

unpacking the strategies

mental strategies

partitioning into hundreds, tens and ones

putting the larger number first

adding or subtracting a near multiple of 100 (or 1000), and adjusting

expectations

Year 5: add a three-digit multiple of 10 to a three-digit number, without crossing the hundreds boundary

Year 6: add a three-digit multiple of 10 to any three-digit number

Years 5 and 6: count up from any three-digit number to the next multiple of 100

Introduce these strategies during the challenge as appropriate.

partitioning into hundreds, tens and ones

Remind children that partitioning is a reliable method of addition that can be used to add any pair of numbers – although sometimes other methods are quicker. Children can aim to do calculations like these quickly and without any written notes at all. Where appropriate, tell children to jot down intermediate numbers if they are likely to lose track.

putting the larger number first

Remind children to put the larger number first, and point out that an effective approach is to partition only the smaller number.

$120 + 324 = \square$

$324 + 120 = 324 + 100 + 20$

$= 424 + 20 = 444$

$537 + 740 = \square$

$740 + 537 = 740 + 500 + 30 + 7$

$= 1240 + 30 + 7 = 1270 + 7$

$= 1277$

adding or subtracting a near multiple of 100 (or 1000), and adjusting

When one of the numbers is close to a multiple of 100 (by a margin of 30), encourage children to add the near multiple of 100 and adjust the answer. Demonstrate this on an empty number line.

$742 + 680 = 742 + 700 - 20$

$= 1442 - 20 = 1422$

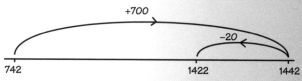

Children can use this method to check the final answer is correct. They work backwards using subtractions.

$1422 - 680 = 1422 - 700 + 20$

$= 722 + 20 = 742$

additional strategies

using the relationship between addition and subtraction   (see challenge 6)

finding a difference by counting up through the next multiple of 10, 100 or 1000   (see challenges 2, 6 and 8)

Two by three
setting out the challenge

getting started

Draw two empty 2 × 3 grids on the board. Introduce the 'Two by three' challenge by inviting two volunteers to play a demonstration game. Their aim is to make two three-digit numbers whose total is greater than the other player's. Each player rolls the dice in turn and writes that digit in one of their boxes.

When the boxes are full, invite methods for adding the two numbers mentally and write up the solutions. The player with the higher total wins.

pairs

Each child draws a 2 × 3 grid and writes zero in one of the right-hand boxes. They take it in turns to roll the dice and decide which box to write the digit in, with the same aim: to make two numbers with a total higher than their partner's.

Play five rounds before declaring the winner.

concluding

Collect in some of the number pairs produced in the 'Two by three' challenge. Ask the children to add them, explaining their mental processes as they do so. Encourage children to check the results using subtraction.

"Which bits of those numbers are you going to deal with first?"

"Can you tell by looking at the two numbers whether the total will be more or less than 500?"

an activity for pairs

0–9 dice or spinner per pair

round 1

Player One

7	4	0
1	3	7

Player Two

6	8	0
7	4	2

Player One
877
check
877 − 740 = 137

Player Two
1422
check
1422 − 680 = 742

Player Two wins

variations

■ Play the same game using decimal numbers.

■ Arrange digits 1 to 6 in the boxes to make two numbers with a total as near as possible to 500.

On target

unpacking the strategies

mental strategies

using known number facts and place value

finding a difference by counting up through the next multiple of 10, 100 or 1000

expectations

Year 5: add or subtract a single-digit multiple of 100 to or from any three-digit number

Year 6: add or subtract a single-digit multiple of 100 to or from any four-digit number

Introduce these strategies during the challenge as appropriate.

using known number facts and place value

When children carry out the initial subtraction in 'On target', tell them to focus on the thousands and hundreds (the tens and ones are straightforward).

$$500 - 251 = (500 - 200) - 51$$
$$= 300 - 51 = 249$$

With 4516 – 700 it is helpful to think of 4500 as 45 hundreds.

$$4516 - 700 = 4500 - 700 + 16$$
$$= 3800 + 16 = 3816$$

Children can aim to do calculations like these quickly and without written notes if possible.

finding a difference by counting up through the next multiple of 10, 100 or 1000

Remind children that, to find how close their answers are to the target, they must find the difference between their answer and 300 (or 3000 for Year 6). Explain that when their answer is greater than the target, subtracting the target will be the best option.

320 take away 300 equals 20

3816 take away 3000 equals 816

But when their answer is smaller than the target number, it is best to count up from their answer to the target to find the difference.

$$251 + \boxed{} = 300$$
$$2816 + \boxed{} = 3000$$

You can use an empty number line to model this, or a spike abacus.

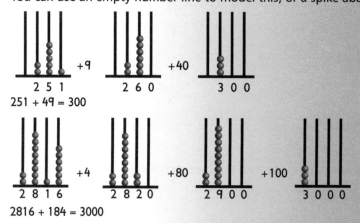

251 + 49 = 300

2816 + 184 = 3000

additional strategies

identifying near doubles   (see challenge 4)

using the relationship between addition and subtraction   (see challenge 6)

On target

setting out the challenge

getting started

Write this sequence of boxes on the board. (For Year 6 add a fourth box on the left-hand side for the thousands.)

The aim of the 'On target' challenge is to complete the numbers to achieve a difference as near as possible to 300 (or 3000 for Year 6). Roll a 0–9 dice and call out the digit. Ask the class which box to write the digit in.

When the two numbers have been made, invite methods for finding the difference between them mentally and write up the solution. Ask the children how close this answer is to the target number, and write this down too.

pairs

The children draw similar boxes of their own. They use the same digits that you have just used as a class, and try to re-arrange them to make numbers with a difference that is even closer to 300 (or 3000 for Year 6). Then they rearrange the digits to find the difference that is furthest from 300.

concluding

Invite children to share their results, and establish which solution comes closest to the target.

"Can you explain why you put the 1 in that position?"

"How can we tell which of these two numbers is closer to 3000?"

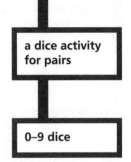
a dice activity for pairs

0–9 dice

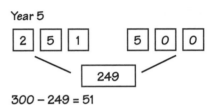
Year 5

$300 - 249 = 51$

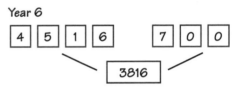
Year 6

$3816 - 3000 = 816$

variations

■ Pick cards from a set of 0–9 number cards and arrange them in these boxes to make two numbers with a difference as near as possible to 300.

■ Arrange the digits 2, 4, 6, 8 in these boxes to make two decimal numbers with a difference as near as possible to 1.

Ask the audience

unpacking the strategies

mental strategies

partitioning into
thousands, hundreds
and tens

adding or subtracting
a near multiple of 100
(or 1000), and adjusting

expectations

Year 5: add or subtract
any pair of three-digit
multiples of 10

Year 6: add or subtract
any pair of four-digit
multiples of 100

Introduce these strategies during the challenge as appropriate.

partitioning into thousands, hundreds and tens

Remind children that partitioning involves considering the value of
each digit – adding thousands to thousands, hundreds to hundreds,
tens to tens and ones to ones – and then combining the results.
Check that the children know to keep the first number complete
and only partition the second (smaller) number.

$450 + 230 = 450 + 200 + 30$

$= 650 + 30$

$= 680$

$4700 + 2400 = 4700 + 2000 + 400$

$= 6700 + 400$

$= 6700 + 300 + 100$

$= 7000 + 100$

$= 7100$

adding or subtracting a near multiple of 100 (or 1000), and adjusting

Tell children that rounding numbers up or down to multiples of 100
(or 1000), then compensating as necessary by adding or subtracting
the extra tens (or hundreds) is an effective strategy. Show how to
use this method with numbers between 10 and 30 away from a
multiple of 100.

$240 + 470$

470 is 30 away from 500

$240 + 470 = 240 + 500 - 30$

$= 740 - 30$

$= 710$

This method works equally well with multiples of 1000.

$2900 + 1300$

2900 is 100 away from 3000

$2900 + 1300 = 3000 + 1300 - 100$

$= 4300 - 100$

$= 4200$

additional strategies

putting the larger number first   (see challenge 1)

identifying near doubles   (see challenge 4)

Ask the audience

setting out the challenge

getting started

Write a calculation on the board and ask the children to work in pairs
to do it. (For Year 6 use multiples of 1000.)

Note the methods used and, where possible, select children to explain
to the class how the calculation might be worked out by adding a
multiple of 10 and adjusting, and by partitioning.

Discuss why these methods might be best for the numbers involved.

pairs

Write an array of numbers on the board, and give pairs of children
sheets of paper with two headings: 'partitioning' and 'adding the
nearest multiple of 100 (or 1000)'.

In pairs, the children create ten different addition calculations, using
a combination of the numbers written up – first multiplying each
number by 10 (or 100 for Year 6).

When the pairs come to add each of their ten calculations, they need
to decide which of the two methods to use for each addition and then
to record the calculation under one heading (or, if appropriate, both
headings) on their sheets of paper.

If they strongly prefer another method, such as using 'near doubles',
they should make a note of that, separately.

class

Invite children to share several of their calculations (but not their
workings) with the class and to 'ask the audience' which method
would be a good way of arriving at the solution. Then the children
can explain why they chose the particular method they used.

concluding

"Was partitioning the only method to use here? Was it the best
method?"

"What kind of numbers do you think are best suited for the method
of adding a near multiple of 10?"

$590 + 730$
$= 730 + 590$
$= 730 + 600 - 10$
$= 1330 - 10$
$= 1320$
or
$590 + 730$
$= 730 + 500 + 90$
$= 1230 + 90$
$= 1230 + 70 + 20$
$= 1300 + 20$
$= 1320$

69	81	34
27	19	71
45	52	90

$690 + 900$
$810 + 710$
$340 + 340$
$270 + 450$
$190 + 270$
$710 + 690$
$810 + 190$
$520 + 450$
$340 + 270$
$690 + 810$

variations

■ Instead of adding pairs of numbers, find the difference.

■ Add three-digit numbers that are not multiples of 10.

■ Adapt the two methods to working with decimal numbers.

The golden triangle
unpacking the strategies

Introduce these strategies during the challenge as appropriate.

mental strategies

using the relationship between multiplication and addition

looking for pairs that make 10 or a multiple of 10

identifying near doubles

using the relationship between multiplication and addition

Tell children that, when adding several numbers with the same tens digit, they can use their knowledge of multiplication.

25 + 26 + 27

is equivalent to

(20 × 3) + 5 + 6 + 7

= 60 + 18 = 78

In this way the tens can be dealt with simply, allowing children to focus on adding the ones.

looking for pairs that make 10 or a multiple of 10

Remind children of the strategy of looking for numbers that total 10 or a multiple of 10.

24 + 25 + 26

= 25 + 24 + 26

= 25 + 50 = 75

expectations

Year 5: add three two-digit multiples of 10

add three two-digit numbers with a total less than 100

Year 6: add four two-digit multiples of 10

add four two-digit numbers that are close

identifying near doubles

Explain to children that when they have a string of three consecutive numbers, they can choose from two different near doubles.

44 + 45 + 46

= (44 + 45) + 46

= (double 44 + 1) + 46

= 88 + 1 + 46

= 89 + 46

= 90 + 46 − 1

= 136 − 1 = 135

or

44 + (45 + 46)

= 44 + (double 45 + 1)

= 44 + 90 + 1

= 134 + 1 = 135

Discuss which the children think is more efficient.

additional strategies

partitioning into hundreds, tens and ones   (see challenge 1)

The golden triangle

setting out the challenge

getting started

Write a two-digit number (25, for example) on the board, and ask the class for the next two numbers.

Arrange the numbers in a triangle and invite suggestions for different ways to add the three numbers. The aim is to look for the most economical ways of adding. Repeat, if needed, this time using a two-digit number (and the two consecutive numbers) suggested by one of the children.

pairs

Each player secretly chooses three consecutive numbers, works out the total and gives their partner a triangle showing only the total: their partner has to work out what the three consecutive numbers are. When they have finished, they exchange triangles and share their solutions (and methods), to check each other's work, including checking that the three numbers are consecutive. The first round of 'The golden triangle' is over when they reach this point.

Children play three rounds of 'The golden triangle'.

concluding

Invite selected children to share one of their additions with the class, and explain their method. Discuss how children estimated the three consecutive numbers they wanted to try.

"What do you do in your head when you add three forties?"

"The total is 99. Which three numbers should I put in the triangle?"

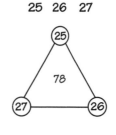

an addition activity for pairs

pencil and paper

round 1
Player One

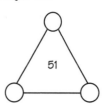

Player Two

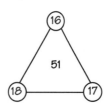

Player One

Player Two

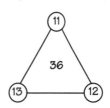

variations

■ Add strings of four consecutive numbers and use a 'silver square'.   47 + 48 + 49 + 50

■ Add strings of numbers that differ by 2, 10 or 100.   32 + 34 + 36

■ Add strings of decimal numbers.   1·9 + 2·9 + 3·9

Go digital

unpacking the strategies

Introduce these strategies during the challenge as appropriate.

mental strategies

adding or subtracting a near multiple of 10, and adjusting

finding a small difference by counting up

expectations

Year 5: add and subtract numbers less than 10 with one decimal place, such as 5·7 + 2·5

add and subtract numbers less than 1 with two decimal places, such as 0·17 + 0·25

Year 6: add and subtract numbers to one or two decimal places, such as 0·17 + 5·2

add and subtract pairs of decimal fractions each less than 1 and with up to two decimal places, such as 0·7−0·26

adding or subtracting a near multiple of 10, and adjusting

Explain to children that the strategy of rounding up or down and then adjusting the answer works with decimal numbers, just as it does with whole numbers. Demonstrate this by giving them a calculation in whole numbers and then using it to create a calculation in decimal form.

76 + 42

= 80 + 42 − 4

= 122 − 4 = 122 − 2 − 2

= 120 − 2 = 118

Now create a related calculation involving decimals (remembering to establish the value of each digit).

7·6 + 4·2

8·0 + 4·2 − 0·4

= 12·2 − 0·4

= 12·2 − 0·2 − 0·2

= 12·0 − 0·2 = 11·8

finding a small difference by counting up

Use an empty number line to demonstrate to children how they can use this strategy with decimal numbers as well as with whole numbers.

9·2 − 7·3 = ☐

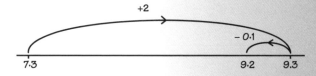

9·2 − 7·3 = 1·9

additional strategies

using known number facts and place value   **(see challenges 2 and 7)**

using the relationship between addition and subtraction   **(see challenge 6)**

Go digital

setting out the challenge

getting started

Write an addition with decimal numbers on the board, using empty boxes instead of digits.

Year 5 $\square . \square + \square . \square$

Year 6 $\square . \square\square + \square . \square\square$

Call a volunteer to the front to roll the dice, read out the number and decide which box to write the digit in. Repeat this with several different children, until you have written up an addition calculation.

Check that the class know the value of each digit in the two numbers, before working out the calculation with them.

Repeat this with a subtraction calculation.

pairs

Each pair needs a 0–9 dice. They draw up an 'addition' as on the board, with empty boxes instead of digits, and roll the dice to generate numbers to put in the boxes. Each child, though, has different aims – one is aiming for a total above 9·2 and the other for a total below it.

Between them they roll the dice and both use that score to fill in one of their empty boxes. When all the boxes are filled, they find the total and then the difference between their total and 9·2. The winner of that round is the player with the smaller difference. (If their score is not above or below 9·2 as required, they lose that round.)

Children play for three rounds. The best out of three is overall winner of the game.

concluding

Go over some of the calculations that children created. Focus on the range of strategies used and discuss their benefits and disadvantages.

"Is the answer going to be more than 9·2? How do you know?"

"Which part of the calculation did you start with? Why?"

---

a dice game for pairs using decimal notation

0–9 dice per pair

Year 5 $\square . \square - \square . \square$

or $0 . \square\square - 0 . \square\square$

Year 6 $0 . \square\square - 0 . \square$

round 1

Player One

7·6   4·2

7·6 + 4·2 = 11·8

11·8 − 9·2 = 2·6

Player Two

2·7   4·6

2·7 + 4·6 = 7·3

9·2 − 7·3 = 1·9

Player Two wins

---

variations

■ In each round the winning player scores the difference between the total and the 'turning point' number. After three rounds they tot up their scores to find the overall winner.

Mix and match

unpacking the strategies

mental strategies

finding a difference by counting up through the next multiple of 10, 100 or 1000

using the relationship between addition and subtraction

expectations

Years 5 and 6: find what to add to a three-digit number to make the next higher multiple of 100

add three or more three-digit multiples of 100

Introduce these strategies during the challenge as appropriate.

finding a difference by counting up through the next multiple of 10, 100 or 1000

Show children how to deal with one part of the number at a time, starting with the lowest value digit.

368 ⟶ 400

368 + 2 = 370

370 + 30 = 400

368 + 32 = 400

using the relationship between addition and subtraction

Check that children are aware that, when making a three-digit number up to its next higher multiple of 100, the calculation they do can be seen either as an addition or a subtraction.

368 + ☐ = 400

400 − 368 = ☐

Demonstrate the addition on an empty number line.

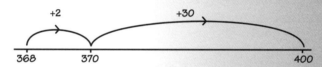

Show how this approach can work either way by demonstrating this on a different calculation as a subtraction.

502 + ☐ = 600

600 − 502 = ☐

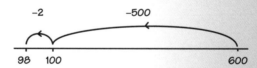

so 600 − 502 = 98

Encourage children to use addition (or subtraction) to check their calculations.

502 + 98

= 502 + 100 − 2

= 602 − 2

= 600

additional strategies

partitioning into hundreds, tens and ones   (see challenge 1)

Mix and match

setting out the challenge

getting started

Write some three-digit numbers on the board and ask the children to tell you, in each case, what is the next higher multiple of 100. Then discuss with them possible methods for finding the difference between each number and the next higher multiple of 100.

624 ⟶ 700

382 ⟶ 400

a class activity for pairs of children

pairs

Using their blank cards, children (working in pairs) choose nine three-digit numbers to write on the cards; then, on the remaining cards, they write in the numbers needed to make each number up to its nearest multiple of 100.

378	251	362
817	428	998
188	456	677

eighteen blank cards or slips of paper per pair

Children use the cards to play the 'Mix and match' challenge. They put their cards face down on the table and take turns to pick two cards to turn face up; if the cards total a multiple of 100 they keep them and, if not, they turn them face down again. They continue like this until all the number pairs are won.

22	49	38
83	72	2
12	44	23

Each child now picks their 'best' three pairs (those with the highest multiples of 100) and finds the total of these cards. The player with the higher score wins the game. Children will almost certainly need to write down the value of their pairs, but as these all total a multiple of 100 they should be able to add up their three best pairs in their heads.

Player One

400 500 700

total 1600

Player Two

900 400 500

total 1800

Player Two wins

class

Find out which children got the highest scores and which the lowest. Read out the three-digit numbers and ask the class to tell you the complement to the next higher multiple of 100 for each number.

concluding

Discuss the methods children used to add their three best pairs.

"How can you tell immediately that 362 and 44 don't add up to a multiple of 100?"

"Which bit of the number do you like to deal with first? Why?"

variations

■ Find the total of all your cards, not just the best three pairs.

■ Use single-digit and two-digit numbers and make them up to the next higher multiple of 10.

34 and 6 or 63 and 7

■ Use two-digit numbers and make them up to 100.

34 and 66 or 63 and 37

■ Use three-digit numbers and make them up to 1000.

346 and 654 or 632 and 368

As luck would have it

unpacking the strategies

mental strategies

using partitioning to add or subtract pairs of decimal numbers

using known number facts and place value

finding a small difference by counting up

expectations

Year 5: find what to add to a decimal number with ones and tenths to make the next higher whole number

Year 6: find what to add to a decimal number with ones, tenths and hundredths to make the next higher whole number

Introduce these strategies during the challenge as appropriate.

using partitioning to add or subtract pairs of decimal numbers

Remind children that if they can add and subtract whole numbers, they can also add and subtract decimal numbers. Encourage them to pay attention to the position of the digits and to partition the smaller number.

$3·7 + 4·2$

$= 4·2 + 3·7$

$= 4·2 + 3 + 0·7$

$= 7·2 + 0·7$

$= 7·9$

using known number facts and place value

Show children how they can apply their knowledge of number bonds (single-digit pairs such as $6 + 4 = 10$ or two-digit pairs such as $75 + 25 = 100$) to decimal numbers as well as whole numbers.

$5·25 + \square = 6$

$25 + 75 = 100$

$0·25 + 0·75 = 1$

(25 hundredths added to 75 hundredths makes 100 hundredths)

so $5·25 + 0·75 = 6$

Remind children that they can use their knowledge of place value to check their answers.

$7·2 + 0·8 = 8$

check: $72 + 8 = 80$

finding a small difference by counting up

Demonstrate on an empty number line how to find a decimal difference by counting up (and adjusting if appropriate).

$7·71 + \square = 8$

$7·71 + 0·29 = 8$

additional strategies

putting the larger number first   (see challenge 1)

using the relationship between addition and subtraction   (see challenge 6)

As luck would have it

setting out the challenge

calculations
finding what to add to a decimal number to make the next higher whole number

a game using decimal notation for pairs

spinner showing more/less per pair

getting started

First, write four decimal numbers on the board and invite children to tell you the next higher whole number for each one. (Go to two decimal places with Year 6.)

4·5   7·7
5·9   2·4

Now demonstrate 'As luck would have it' with two volunteers. Each player writes two decimal numbers on the board. The other player has to add them, record the total and give the calculation back to their partner, who then notes down the next higher whole number and works out the difference between their total and that whole number. One player spins the spinner to decide who is the winner of that round. If it says 'more', the player with the larger difference wins the round; if it says 'less', the player with the smaller difference wins.

demonstration round

Player One
4·2   3·7
total 7·9

Player Two
6·5   3·9
total 10·4

pairs

After pairs of children have played three to five rounds of 'As luck would have it', ask them to count up how many rounds they have won and establish the winner in each pair.

Player One
7·9 + 0·1 = 8
difference 0·1

Player Two
10·4 + 0·6 = 11
difference 0·6

class

Invite children to tell you some of the number pairs they worked with, and check the totals with the class. Concentrate attention on how to make the totals up to the next higher whole number. Discuss the methods used, and introduce any that deserve mention but have not been suggested.

spinner: greater

Player Two wins

concluding

"The number is 3·7 (or for Year 6, 3·77). How many ones and how many tenths (or hundredths) is that?"

"If 89 needs 1 to make it up to 90, how much does 8·9 need to make it up to 9?"

variations

■ Start with whole numbers before moving on to decimals.

■ The greater difference always scores the point – prompting the children to think in general terms about what kind of number pairs produce large differences.

The diamond run

unpacking the strategies

mental strategies

finding a difference by counting up through the next multiple of 10, 100 or 1000

subtracting a near multiple of 10, 100 or 1000, and adjusting

expectations

Year 5: subtract a four-digit number just less than a multiple of 1000 from a four-digit number just more than a multiple of 1000, such as 5003 – 3998

Year 6: subtract any four-digit number from a multiple of 1000, such as 6000 – 3842

Introduce these strategies during the challenge as appropriate.

finding a difference by counting up through the next multiple of 10, 100 or 1000

Remind children that, when they are working out the difference between two numbers, they can check whether the numbers are either side of a multiple of 10, 100 or 1000. Knowing this could make their task a lot easier.

All the following calculations can be done easily, by counting up through multiples of 10, 100, 1000 or 10 000.

72 – 69

709 – 299

5010 – 2989

72 001 – 71 991

The numbers in 'The diamond run' are all thousands. Model on a number line how to make the lower number up to a multiple of 1000; then add on enough to make it up to the higher number.

5003 – 2992

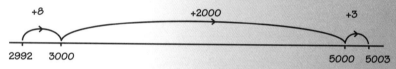

$$5003 - 2992 = 8 + 2000 + 3 = 2000 + 8 + 3 = 2011$$

With a calculation such as 5000 – 3648, point out that an efficient strategy is to count up from the smaller to the larger number.

$$2 + 50 + 300 + 1000 = 1352$$

subtracting a near multiple of 10, 100 or 1000, and adjusting

Point out to children that, when they need to subtract a single digit from a multiple of 1000, they can subtract 10 and adjust.

$$5000 - 8 = 5000 - 10 + 2$$
$$= 4090 + 2$$
$$= 4092$$

If appropriate, give children practice in counting forwards and backwards in tens.

4900, 4910, 4920... 4990, 5000, 5010

5010, 5000, 4990... 4920, 4910, 4900

additional strategies

using known number facts and place value   (see challenges 2 and 7)

using the relationship between addition and subtraction   (challenges 6)

The diamond run

setting out the challenge

an addition and subtraction activity for pairs

worksheets showing blank 'diamond run' sequences

1–9 dice or 1–9 spinners

getting started

Give children practice in counting down in ones and then tens from numbers above a multiple of 1000, crossing the 1000 boundary.

5003 5002 5001 5000 4999 4998 4997 4996

5031 5021 5011 5001 4991 4981

Demonstrate 'The diamond run' challenge on the board. First draw a sequence of empty boxes, circles and a diamond. Then roll a dice (or spin a spinner) to generate four numbers, and write these in the circles, in any order. (For Year 6, put a zero in the lower left circle and ask the children to place two numbers, in any order, in the lower right circle.)

Ask children to help you multiply the number in the top circles by 1000; add one of the dice numbers to the multiple in the top left box and subtract the other dice number from the multiple in the top right box; then find the difference between these two numbers and record the answer.

pairs

Individuals roll dice and arrange the numbers generated in the circles on their worksheet, and work through the 'diamond run' sequence, but stop before working out the difference. They write only the two numbers on a separate strip of paper and pass it to their partner, for them to work out the difference. When both children have worked out each other's calculation, they check the calculations together by adding the answer to the smaller number.

concluding

Use children's work to write pairs of numbers on the board and ask the class to work out the difference. Now ask children to work backwards to find out the four dice numbers that were written in the circles. Discuss what connections the children might have noticed.

"What different methods might you use to work out the difference between the two numbers?"

"The two numbers are either side of 200 and the difference between them is 6. What might the numbers be?"

variations

■ Multiply the first number by 100 not 1000.

■ Roll a 1–6 dice to keep the numbers small.

■ Roll a 1–12 dice for more challenging numbers.

■ Generate three (instead of two) numbers for the lower right circle.

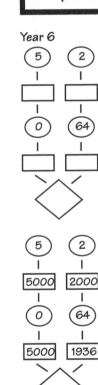

Multiplication and division

a set of sixteen challenges ▪

calculations

multiplying any two-digit number by 50 or 25

multiplying any two-digit number by any single digit

multiplying two- or three-digit numbers by multiples of 10 or 100

finding factors using fractions

doubling and halving whole numbers

multiplying a decimal fraction by any single digit

finding percentages of numbers

multiplying any two-digit multiple of 10 or three-digit multiple of 100 by a single digit

dividing multiples of 100 by 10, 100 or 1000

dividing any whole number by 10 or 100, giving any remainder as a decimal

halving a three-digit multiple of 10

halving a decimal fraction less than 1

multiplying a two-digit number by 10 or 100

multiplying a decimal fraction by 10 or 100

finding squares of numbers

strategies

using doubling or halving, starting from known number facts

doubling or halving by dealing with the most significant digits first

doubling one number and halving the other

multiplying by 50 by multiplying by 100 and then halving

multiplying by 25 by multiplying by 100, halving and then halving again

multiplying by 15 by multiplying by 10, halving and then adding the two answers

finding sixths, twelfths and twentieths by halving

using factors

using closely related facts

partitioning

using the relationship between multiplication and division

using known number facts and place value

using place value to multiply and divide by 10, 100 or 1000

adding or subtracting a near multiple of 10, and adjusting

■ this strategy is described in detail here

☐ this strategy is referred to as an additional option here

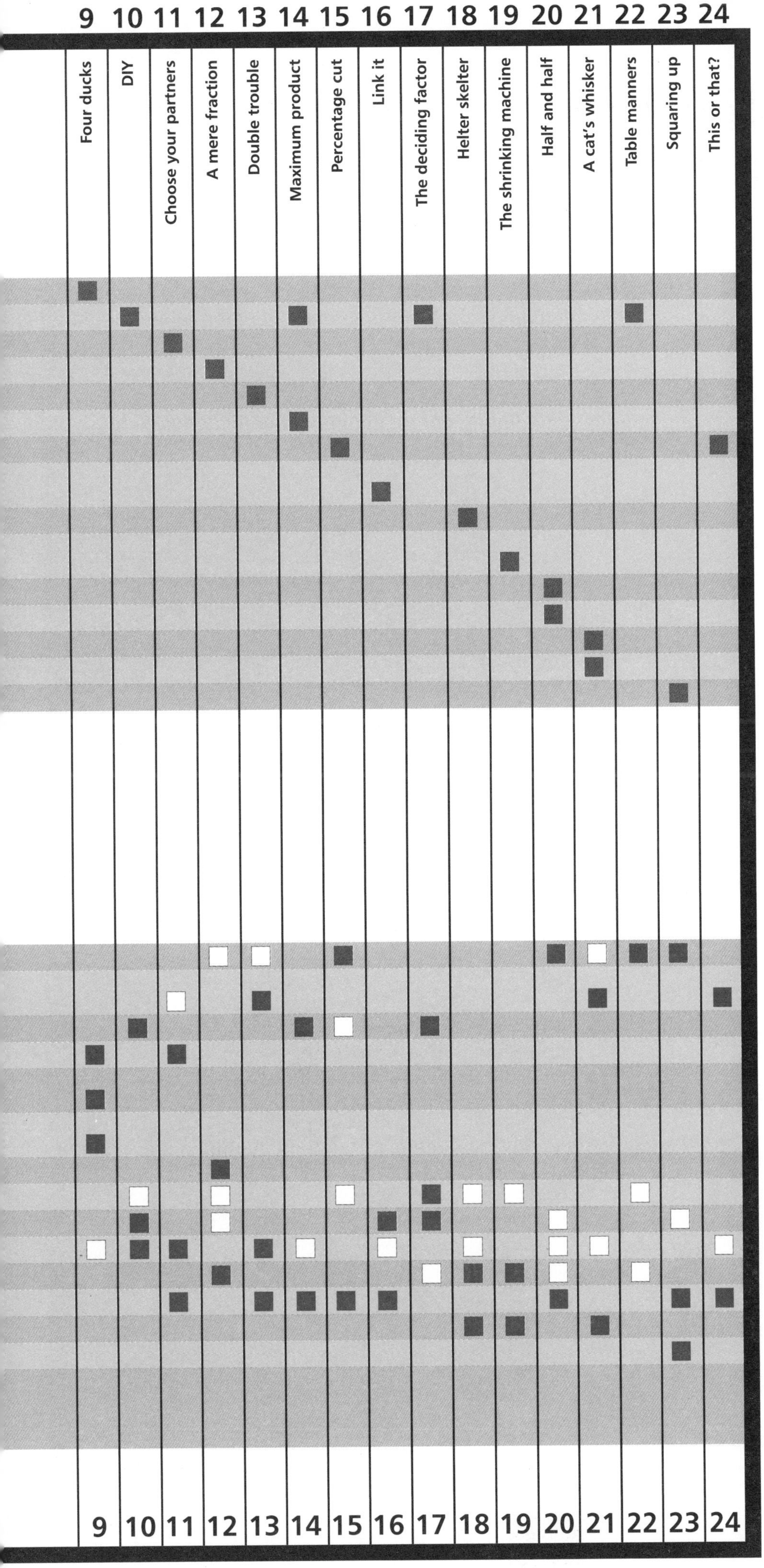

9 10 11 12 13 14 15 16 17 18 19 20 21 22 23 24
Four ducks
DIY
Choose your partners
A mere fraction
Double trouble
Maximum product
Percentage cut
Link it
The deciding factor
Helter skelter
The shrinking machine
Half and half
A cat's whisker
Table manners
Squaring up
This or that?
9 10 11 12 13 14 15 16 17 18 19 20 21 22 23 24

Four ducks

unpacking the strategies

mental strategies

multiplying by 50 by multiplying by 100 and then halving

multiplying by 25 by multiplying by 100, halving and then halving again

multiplying by 15 by multiplying by 10, halving and then adding the two answers

expectations

Year 5: multiply any two-digit number by 50

Year 6: multiply any two-digit number by 25

Introduce these strategies during the challenge as appropriate.

multiplying by 50 by multiplying by 100 and then halving

Remind children that to multiply a number by 50 you can multiply by 5 and then by 10. This can be a quick method, when you are dealing with small numbers.

$6 \times 50 = 6 \times 5 \times 10 = 30 \times 10$

$= 300$

With harder numbers (such as are used in the 'Four ducks' challenge) a more effective approach is to multiply by 100 and then halve the result.

$17 \times 100 = 1700$

so $17 \times 50 = 1700 \div 2$

$= 850$

Remind children that to multiply by 100 they have to move the digits two spaces to the left.

multiplying by 25 by multiplying by 100, halving and then halving again

Show children that, to multiply by 25, they can follow the pattern for multiplying by 50, then halve the result.

$17 \times 100 = 1700$

$17 \times 50 = 850$

$17 \times 25 = 425$

Point out that this is the same as multiplying by 100 and then dividing by 4.

multiplying by 15 by multiplying by 10, halving and then adding the two answers

Point out to the children that multiplying by 15 is straightforward. Set out the calculation to make it explicit how halving a multiple of 10 is the same as multiplying by 5.

$44 \times 10 = 440$

$44 \times 5 = 220$

$44 \times 15 = 660$

additional strategies

partitioning   (see challenges 10, 11 and 13)

Four ducks

setting out the challenge

getting started

Multiply the numbers on the dice by 15 and 50 (for Year 6, by 15 and 25) and write the results on the board.

225	255	285
345	555	1080
750	850	950
1150	1850	3600

a multiplication
game for pairs

The children draw a 4 × 4 grid and write, in any order, the numbers from the board (one in each box), then choose four of the numbers to write again in the spare boxes.

225	850	255	285
255	1080	750	1150
850	950	1850	3600
345	750	1850	555

Roll the dice and spin the spinner, and call out the numbers. Invite one of the children to multiply these together and to tell the class the answer. Discuss the methods children can use to do these multiplications and encourage them to choose strategies that require little or no recording en route.

When the product is agreed, any child who has that number on their grid can cross it through. Continue until one child (or several) has crossed through a line of four numbers (vertical, horizontal or diagonal).

demonstration
dice showing
15, 17, 19, 23,
37, 72
dice showing
16, 18, 21, 24,
35, 63
(or other two-
digit numbers)

Year 5
spinner
showing 15
and 50

Year 6
spinner
showing 15
and 25

pairs

Write up the two spinner numbers and the six new dice numbers. Children work in pairs and record all the multiplications to be found from multiplying a spinner number by a dice number. Play the game again, until someone has their 'four ducks in a row'.

concluding

Choose several multiplications and discuss the strategies used.

"How can you multiply a number by 15 in your head?"

"How can you use the last digit as a quick check that your multiplication looks right?"

round 1

spinner: 15
dice: 19
15 x 19
= 285

spinner: 50
dice: 15
50 x 15
= 750

spinner: 50
dice: 23
50 x 23
= 1150

spinner: 15
dice: 37
15 x 37
= 555

spinner: 15
dice: 15
15 x 15
= 225

spinner: 50
dice: 72
50 x 72
= 3600

four ducks in a row!

variations

- Use a spinner with other numbers, such as 12 and 15; or a dice numbered, say, 10, 12, 15, 20, 25, 100.

- Use a spinner with other numbers which suggest other strategies, such as 19 (use the method of multiplying by 20 and adjusting) and 30 (use the method of multiplying by 10, then by 3).

DIY

unpacking the strategies

mental strategies

doubling one number and halving the other

partitioning

using closely related facts

expectations

Year 5: derive the 11, 12, 14, 21 times tables from known facts

Year 6: derive the 15, 16, 18, 19, 25 times tables from known facts

Introduce these strategies during the challenge as appropriate.

doubling one number and halving the other

Show children how this method is useful when either number in the multiplication has a double or half which is 'easy' to multiply.

$18 \times 5 = 9 \times 10$

18 is not an easy number to multiply by, but it is an even number, so it can be halved. When you halve the 18 you have to double the 5.

$18 \times 5 = 9 \times 2 \times 5$

$= 9 \times 10$

$= 90$

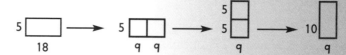

partitioning

Show how you can multiply by 11 or 12 by multiplying by 10 and then 1 (or 2). This is known as the distributive law; children do not need to learn this term, although they will absorb and understand the principles.

$7 \times 11 = 7 \times (10 + 1)$

$= (7 \times 10) + (7 \times 1)$

$= 70 + 7 = 77$

7 | 10 | 1 |

$9 \times 12 = 9 \times (10 + 2)$

$= (9 \times 10) + (9 \times 2)$

$= 90 + 18 = 108$

9 | 10 | 2 |

using closely related facts

Remind children that often a new multiplication fact can be derived from an easier one. For example, to multiply 19 by 8, multiply by 20 and subtract 8.

$19 \times 8 = (20 - 1) \times 8$

$= (20 \times 8) - (1 \times 8)$

$= 160 - 8$

$= 152$

additional strategies

using factors

(see challenge 17)

DIY

setting out the challenge

calculations
multiplying any
two digit number
by any single digit

getting started

Draw a grid on the board.

	x1	x2	x3	x4	x5	x6	x7	x8	x9	x10
13										

Talk to the children about how any multiplication table can be derived using doubling, halving and addition. Write 13 in the first empty box of the grid and ask the class to work out double 13, then ten thirteens. Write these in.

Now ask the class for other facts that can be worked out from these two results, using doubling, halving or addition. Children may suggest adding another 13 to 26 to get 13×3; halving 13×10 to get 13×5; and doubling 13×2 to get 13×4.

Continue to complete the grid as the children make suggestions. Ask children for alternative strategies for checking each fact. If, for example, the children halved 13×10 to get 13×5, they can check the result by adding 13 to the answer to 13×4.

$13 \times 10 = 130$

so

$13 \times 5 = 65$

$13 \times 4 = 52$

so

$13 \times 5 = 52 + 13 = 65$

a class activity
constructing a
multiplication
table followed
by pairs work

2 × 11 grid
per pair

pairs

Give each pair of children a grid and a two-digit number, and ask them to derive the multiplication table in the same way, or using any other strategies they choose. For Year 5, appropriate tables might be 11, 12, 14, 21. For Year 6, try 15, 16, 18, 19, 25.

concluding

Look at the patterns of the digits in each table and talk about how these can be used to check for errors in the table.

"What pattern do the final digits make in the 12 times table?"

"What do you notice about the tens and hundreds digits in the 15 times table? Read the numbers out and tell us what is missing. Can you see the pattern?"

variations

- Revise the tables below 10 by recreating them, using doubling, halving and addition. For example, to create the 8 times table write out the 4 times table and double it.

- Talk about methods other than doubling for working out a table. For example, to work out the 19 times table, add the results of the 9 times and 10 times tables.

Choose your partners

unpacking the strategies

mental strategies

using known number facts and place value

multiplying by 50 by multiplying by 100 and then halving

partitioning

expectations

Year 5: multiply any two- or three-digit number by 10 or 100

multiply any two-digit multiple of 10 by a three-digit multiple of 100

Year 6: multiply or divide any whole number by 10 or 100

Introduce these strategies during the challenge as appropriate.

using known number facts and place value

Discuss with the children how using their understanding of place value for the 'Choose your partners' challenge makes the calculations easier to handle.

$15 \times 300 = 15 \times 3 \times 100$

$= 45 \times 100 = 4500$

and

$304 \times 200 = 304 \times 2 \times 100$

$= 608 \times 100 = 60\,800$

When multiplying by 10, 100 or 1000, describe the process as 'moving the digits to the left'. Discourage the idea of 'adding noughts', which is mathematically incorrect and confusing.

multiplying by 50 by multiplying by 100 and then halving

Explore with the children whether it makes any difference if you halve first and then multiply by 100, or multiply by 100 and then halve.

$304 \times 50 = 304 \times 100 \div 2$

$= 30\,400 \div 2 = 15\,200$

It is probably easier to halve first if dealing with an even number. However, children may prefer to multiply by 100 first if working with an odd number.

$47 \times 50 = 47 \times 100 \div 2$

$= 4700 \div 2 = 2350$

partitioning

Show how you can work out multiplication calculations in stages, dealing with the hundreds, tens and ones separately. It is important not to miss out any stage of the calculation.

$215 \times 300 = (200 + 10 + 5) \times 300$

$= (200 \times 300) + (10 \times 300) + (5 \times 300)$

$= (60\,000) + (3000) + (1500) = 64\,500$

300	60 000	3000	1500
	200	10	5

additional strategies

doubling or halving by dealing with the most significant digits first

(see challenges 13, 21 and 24)

Choose your partners

calculations

multiplying two- or three-digit numbers by multiples of 10 or 100

getting started

Write these two circles of numbers on the board.

Ask a child to choose a number from each circle, and write them as a multiplication calculation on the board.

Discuss how to multiply these numbers together, encouraging children to consider several methods where appropriate. Repeat this once or twice and note down the main strategies discussed.

15
176   215
304   340
22   47
55   72
9176

an activity for pairs

pencil and paper

pairs

Each child creates a multiplication problem using one number from each circle, then swaps this with their partner, who must find the solution. They then swap back and check each other's solutions using the same, or a different, method. They do this five times.

10
20   30
50   90
100   200
300   600
1000

concluding

Ask children to volunteer some of the multiplication problems they worked on, and their solutions. Pay attention to the methods, and note on the board any additional strategies you want the children to know about.

"If you multiply a number such as 55 by 100, how many zeros will there be in the answer?"

"If I multiply 22 by 200, might there be a 3 anywhere in the answer? How do you know?"

47 × 20

to multiply by 20, double it then multiply by 10

304 × 50

to multiply by 50, multiply by 100 and halve it

variations

■ Write one of the children's products on the board, together with one of the numbers multiplied, and ask the class to work out the missing number.

55 × ☐ = 1650

■ Use single digits in the first circle and two-digit multiples of 10 or three-digit multiples of 100 in the second.

8 × 70 or 8 × 700

■ Use decimal numbers in the first circle and multiples of 10 in the second.

0·5 × 30 or 1·4 × 70

A mere fraction

unpacking the strategies

Introduce these strategies during the challenge as appropriate.

mental strategies

finding sixths, twelfths and twentieths by halving

using the relationship between multiplication and division

expectations

Year 5: derive facts up to 10 × 10

Year 6: divide two-digit numbers by 6, 12 and 20

finding sixths, twelfths and twentieths by halving

Remind children how to recognise numbers that are divisible by 3. Numbers are divisible by 3 if the digits total 3 or a multiple of 3. For example, 171 is divisible by 3 because $1 + 7 + 1 = 9$.

Once the children know $\frac{1}{3}$ of a number, $\frac{1}{6}$ and $\frac{1}{12}$ can be found by halving.

$\frac{1}{3}$ of 48 is 16

so

$\frac{1}{6}$ of 48 is $16 \div 2 = 8$

$\frac{1}{12}$ of 48 is $8 \div 2 = 4$

Encourage children to find tenths and twentieths for decimal answers. For example, a tenth of 28 is 2·8, and a twentieth is 1·4. If necessary, revise division by 10.

Point out that when you halve an odd number you can choose to represent the answer as a vulgar fraction or a decimal. Half 13 can be written $6\frac{1}{2}$ or 6·5.

using the relationship between multiplication and division

Encourage children to make explicit the connections between the facts they derive: "double 15 is 30 so half of 30 is 15"; "ten twos are 20, so 2 must be a tenth of 20". They can collect a set of 'free facts'.

$10 \times 18 = 180$ so 18 is a tenth of 180

and if 18 is a tenth of 180 then 9 is a twentieth of 180

additional strategies

using closely related facts   (see challenges 10, 16 and 17)

using doubling or halving, starting
from known number facts   (see challenges 15, 20 and 23)

using factors   (see challenge 17)

A mere fraction

setting out the challenge

getting started

Write this list of numbers on the board. Choose one number from the list (for example, 12) and invite the children to suggest 'fraction facts' that can be worked out by halving or by using their knowledge of multiplication facts. Write these on the board.

Do the same with another one or two numbers.

groups

In groups, children use all the numbers from the list, and write down whatever 'fraction facts' they can work out about these numbers. They share out the work between them.

teams

Play a team game between the groups. Write a number on the board, such as 5. Give the groups a short time to write all the 'fraction facts' which have that answer on their whiteboard. At a signal from you, groups hold up their whiteboards. They score one point for each correct fact written. Play several rounds. The team with the highest score wins.

concluding

Collect some of the children's work and discuss the 'fraction facts' they managed to derive and ask how they worked out these facts. Discuss how to recognise the divisibility of numbers by, for example, 2, 5 and 10. (For Year 6, look also at divisibility by 3, 4, 6, 8 and 9.)

"$\frac{1}{6}$ was 5 and $\frac{1}{2}$ was 15. What was the whole?"

"What fraction of 300 is 25? How do you know?"

---

12 15 20 28
32 33 48 60
100 180

$\frac{1}{2}$ of 12 is 6
$\frac{1}{4}$ of 12 is 3
$\frac{1}{3}$ of 12 is 4
$\frac{1}{6}$ of 12 is 2
$\frac{1}{12}$ of 12 is 1
$\frac{1}{10}$ of 12 is 1·2

a team game using fractions

whiteboard per team (or large sheet of paper)

round 1
5

Team A	Team B
$\frac{1}{2}$ of 10 is 5	$\frac{1}{2}$ of 10 is 5
$\frac{1}{4}$ of 20 is 5	$\frac{1}{4}$ of 20 is 5
$\frac{1}{5}$ of 25 is 5	$\frac{1}{10}$ of 50 is 5
$\frac{1}{3}$ of 15 is 5	$\frac{1}{3}$ of 15 is 5
$\frac{1}{6}$ of 30 is 5	$\frac{1}{9}$ of 45 is 5
$\frac{1}{10}$ of 50 is 5	$\frac{1}{12}$ of 60 is 5
$\frac{1}{20}$ of 100 is 5	

Team A: 7 points

Team B: 6 points

Team A wins round 1

---

variations

- Write up a fraction such as $\frac{1}{6}$, and teams write all the calculations for that fraction.

- Find halves, quarters and eighths, and only progress to other facts if you feel confident.

- Stick with just one or two numbers and explore them in depth. Use a calculator to allow more elaborate explorations: "$\frac{1}{100}$ of 180 is 1·8; $\frac{1}{50}$ of 180 is 3·6".

- A game for two children: they swap one or two fraction facts without saying what the number was. The challenge is to work out what the number was.

Double trouble

unpacking the strategies

mental strategies

partitioning

doubling or halving by dealing with the most significant digits first

using known number facts and place value

expectations

Year 5: double any number from 1 to 100, and any multiples of 10 to 1000, and find corresponding halves

Year 6: double any two-digit whole number or decimal, and any multiples of 100 to 10 000, and find corresponding halves

Introduce these strategies during the challenge as appropriate.

partitioning

When children want to double a number, they may 'just know' the answer: double 16 is 32 (no need to partition). However, if they don't just know it, they can double the parts of the number separately, then add the results together. It doesn't matter which part they deal with first.

double 540 equals double 500 plus double 40

= 1000 + 80

= 1080

doubling or halving by dealing with the most significant digits first

Discuss with children how, when partitioning, it is often easier to double the most 'valuable' digit first – that is, the hundreds before the tens, and the tens before the ones.

double 370

double 300 is 600, then add on double 70, which is 140

600 + 140 = 740

The same applies when halving.

halve 270

half 200 is 100, then add on half 70, which is 35

100 + 35 = 135

using known number facts and place value

Show children how to look out for ways of using place value and facts they know to modify a number and adjust. For example, when doubling 156, a short cut is to double the 150 then deal with the ones.

double 156

double 150 is 300

so double 156 = 300 + 12 = 312

When halving 468, all you need do is halve the 460 and then the 8.

half 460 is 230, half 8 is 4, so half 468 is 234

additional strategies

using doubling or halving, starting
from known number facts   **(see challenges 15, 20 and 23)**

Double trouble

setting out the challenge

getting started

Write a number between 1 and 20 on the board. Ask the class to help you first multiply the number by 5 and then double it repeatedly until you reach the first number above 1000.

Ask questions referring back to the numbers on the board. "What is double 35? What are four 70s? What is half of 560? What is an eighth of 1120?"

7
35
70
140
280
560
1120

an activity for pairs

pencil and paper

pairs

Explain that the aim of the 'Double trouble' challenge is to find a starting number that gives an end number closest to 1000. Each child chooses a number from 1 to 20, multiplies it by 5 and then doubles it repeatedly. They continue until they reach the first number above 1000. Then their partner chooses a new number.

Play continues until each child has chosen three numbers. Whoever gets an end number closest to 1000 wins.

Player One	Player Two
8	13
$8 \times 5 = 40$	$13 \times 5 = 65$
$40 \times 2 = 80$	$65 \times 2 = 130$
$80 \times 2 = 160$	$130 \times 2 = 260$
$160 \times 2 = 320$	$260 \times 2 = 520$
$320 \times 2 = 640$	$520 \times 2 = 1040$
$640 \times 2 = 1280$	

concluding

Collect in some answers, focusing on those closest to 1000, and ask for the routes that got the children to those answers. Ask the children to explain their strategies for doubling.

Then start with an end number and ask children to keep halving to try and find the starting number.

"Why did starting at 2 and at 16 both get to 1040?"

"The end number is 1280. What numbers is that divisible by? Can you suggest a starting number?"

Player One	Player Two
15	3
and so on, up to	and so on, up to
$600 \times 2 = 1200$	$960 \times 2 = 1920$

play continues
Player Two wins
with 13

variations

- Start with a decimal number and keep doubling until you pass 50. What kind of numbers turn into whole numbers this way, and what kind continue to include a decimal element? Why?

  $0.7 \rightarrow 1.4 \rightarrow 2.8 \rightarrow 5.6 \rightarrow 11.2 \rightarrow$
  $22.4 \rightarrow 44.8 \rightarrow 89.6$

  $0.5 \rightarrow 1 \rightarrow 2 \rightarrow 4 \rightarrow 8 \rightarrow 16 \rightarrow$
  $32 \rightarrow 64$

- Start with an end number and keep halving to try to find the starting number. Work out all the possible starting numbers that would have produced that number, in the range 1 to 30.

Maximum product

unpacking the strategies

mental strategies

doubling one number
and halving the other

using known number
facts and place value

expectations

Year 5: multiply any
two-digit multiple of
10 by a single digit,
such as 80 × 7

Year 6: multiply any
two-digit number
by a single digit, such
as 42 × 8

multiply a decimal
fraction by a single digit,
such as 2·7 × 6

Introduce these strategies during the challenge as appropriate.

doubling one number and halving the other

Tell children that they can use the doubling and halving strategy with
decimal numbers as well as with whole numbers. Explain that the
first step is to decide which number to double and which to halve.

So, if one of the numbers is 5, you can double it to make 10, because
multiplying by 10 is easy. And then you just halve the other number.

34 × 5 = (34 ÷ 2) × 10 = 17 × 10 = 170

If one of the numbers is 4, halve it (and double the other number).

3·5 × 4 = double 3·5 × 2 = 7 × 2 = 14

Use arrays to demonstrate this.

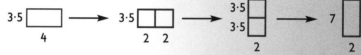

using known number facts and place value

Show children how they can multiply a two-digit decimal number
by a single digit, remembering always to deal with the decimal point.

4·3 × 5 is no harder than 43 × 5

43 × 5 = 40 × 5 and 3 × 5

so 4·3 × 5 = 4 × 5 and 0·3 × 5

= 20 + 1·5 = 21·5

Encourage children to read out the numbers as ones and tenths.

4·3 × 5 is four ones multiplied by 5 and three tenths multiplied by 5

four ones multiplied by 5 is 20

three tenths multiplied by 5 is fifteen tenths, which is one and five tenths,
or 1·5

It may also help to think of 4·3 as ten times smaller than 43. Use the
base 10 blocks to model this. First show 215 with the apparatus and
then ask the children what all the other pieces are worth, if the small
cubes are now worth 0·1 each.

43 × 5 is 215, so 4·3 × 5 must be 10 times smaller, that is 21·5

215

additional strategies

partitioning   (see challenges 10, 11 and 13)

Maximum product

calculations
multiplying any
two-digit number
by any single digit

multiplying a
decimal fraction by
any single digit

getting started

Draw three boxes on the board, separated by a decimal point and a multiplication sign. (For Year 5, omit the decimal point.)

Write the numbers 3, 4 and 5 underneath. Tell the children that you want to arrange these digits in the boxes to make a decimal and a single-digit number, then multiply the two numbers. Your aim is to make as large a product as you can. (For Year 5, multiply a two-digit number by a single digit.)

$$\square . \square \times \square$$
$$3 \quad 4 \quad 5$$

Work systematically with the children to establish the six possible arrangements. Ask the children to help you work out the products of each, and agree which is the largest $(4 \cdot 3 \times 5 = 21 \cdot 5)$.

$3 \cdot 4 \times 5$	$3 \cdot 5 \times 4$
$4 \cdot 3 \times 5$	$4 \cdot 5 \times 3$
$5 \cdot 3 \times 4$	$5 \cdot 4 \times 3$

pairs

Each child chooses three different digits, makes up the six different products possible, then writes the calculations and answers on separate cards and swaps them with their partner, who has to match questions and answers.

$2 \cdot 5 \times 9$	$46 \cdot 8$
$9 \cdot 5 \times 2$	$11 \cdot 8$
$2 \cdot 9 \times 5$	46
$5 \cdot 2 \times 9$	$22 \cdot 5$
$5 \cdot 9 \times 2$	$14 \cdot 5$
$9 \cdot 2 \times 5$	19

concluding

Ask some children to tell the class their choice of numbers and which arrangements gave which size of product. Discuss the methods of multiplication used by the children.

"We have the digits 4, 8 and 6. Has anyone got a feeling which arrangement would make the highest product? Can you say why?"

"Can you make a hypothesis about which arrangement will always make the biggest product?" (The answer you are looking for is: 'middle-sized digit · smallest digit × largest digit'.)

a multiplication
activity for
pairs (using
decimal
notation for
Year 6)

pencil and
paper

variations

- Explore what happens when one of the three digits is zero. Do you get a different answer to 60×5 from the answer to 50×6? What about 61×5 and 51×6? Why is that different?

- Work with three digits (for example, 7, 8 and 9) to make a two- and a single-digit number, and find the largest and smallest product with these same three digits. Generalise about the arrangement of three digits which always gives the largest or smallest product.

Percentage cut

unpacking the strategies

mental strategies

using doubling or halving, starting from known number facts

using known number facts and place value

expectations

Year 5: find percentages (such as 10%, 25% and 50%) of multiples of 10 and 100

Year 6: find more complex percentages of multiples of 10 and 100

Introduce these strategies during the challenge as appropriate.

using doubling or halving, starting from known number facts

Remind children that they can deduce many percentage facts by simply doubling and halving the easy ones they already know.

10% of 500 is 50 (because 10% is the same as $\frac{1}{10}$)

so 20% of 500 is 50 × 2, or 100

and 40% of 500 is 50 × 4 or 200

10% of 200 is 20 (because 10% is the same as $\frac{1}{10}$)

so 5% of 200 is half of 20, or 10

50% of 800 is 400 (because 50% is the same as $\frac{1}{2}$)

so 25% of 800 is half of 400, or 200

using known number facts and place value

Reassure children that large numbers are still straightforward to divide. If it helps, children can work out a division based on a multiple of 10 instead of 100, and then multiply the answer by 10.

50% of 700 = ☐

50% means half, and half of 70 is 35

so half of 700 is 350

Check that children understand the strategy of finding 1% of a number and multiplying. This can provide a valuable check of solutions reached by other methods.

5% of 900 = ☐

10% is 90, so 5% is 45

check this:

1% of 900 is 9

5% is 9 × 5, which is also 45

additional strategies

doubling one number and halving the other

(see challenges 10, 14 and 17)

using factors

(see challenge 17)

Percentage cut

setting out the challenge

**a percentage
game for pairs**

getting started

On the board write some multiples of 10 and 100, and a range of
percentages.

40   500   90   1000   400   300   20

50%   75%   25%   10%   5%   20%

Discuss how children can work out the given percentages of each
number (revising the meaning of 'per cent'). Help individuals to talk
through their thinking as they work out the values: "50% is half and
I know half of 500 is 250"; "10% of 90 is 9 so 20% of 90 must be 18".
Emphasise the strategy of finding a simple percentage such as 10%
– which can be found by dividing by 10 – and doubling or halving
that to find other percentages.

pairs

Children spin the first spinner to find their own personal number,
which is also their initial score. They record these. They then take
turns to spin the percentage spinner, work out that percentage of
their personal number, and subtract that from their score so far. They
continue like this until one player reaches a score of 50 or less; that
player wins the game.

Children play two games.

groups

They then join up with another pair and play two more games.

concluding

Invite a pair or group to give you their recording and talk this through
with the rest of the class, asking children to make explicit their mental
strategies.

"How can you work out 15% of 600?"

"If one player starts with 1000 and the other starts with 500, could
the person with 1000 win? Is this game fair?"

Player One
500
25% of 500 = 125
500 − 125 = 375
5% of 500 = 25
375 − 25 = 350
10% of 500 = 50
350 − 50 = 300
50% of 500 = 250
300 − 250 = 50

Player Two
600
15% of 600 = 90
600 − 90 = 510
50% of 600 = 300
510 − 300 = 210
25% of 600 = 150
210 − 150 = 60

Player One wins

**spinner
showing 500,
600, 700, 800,
900, 1000
per pair**

**spinner
showing 5%,
10%, 15%,
20%, 25%,
50% per pair**

**pencil and
paper**

variations

■ Use fewer percentages.   10%, 20% and 50%

■ Include more complex percentages.   30%, 40% and 45%

■ Continue the game until one player has a score below zero.

■ Start with higher personal numbers, in the thousands or above.   2000, 5000, 8000, 10 000

Link it

unpacking the strategies

mental strategies

using known number facts and place value

using closely related facts

expectations

Year 5: multiply any two-digit multiple of 10 by a single digit

Year 6: multiply any three-digit multiple of 100 by a single digit

Introduce these strategies during the challenge as appropriate.

using known number facts and place value

Discuss with children how the calculations in 'Link it' are no harder than remembering, or working out, the facts in the multiplication tables. The only difference is that they deal with hundreds instead of ones and so the children need to adjust their answers appropriately.

$7 \times 6 = 42$

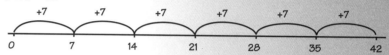

$700 \times 6 = 4200$

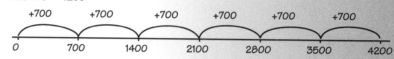

The same applies (for Year 6) when working with decimal numbers.

$0.7 \times 6 = 4.2$

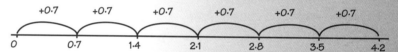

using closely related facts

Remind children that an unknown multiplication fact can be derived from a known one. To multiply 7 by 8 they can multiply 7 by 4, and then double the result. Or they can double 7, three times.

7×8

$7 \times 2 = 14$ so $7 \times 4 = 28$ so $7 \times 8 = 56$

Or to find 3×9, they can double 9 and add on another 9.

3×9

$2 \times 9 = 18$ so $3 \times 9 = 18 + 9 = 27$

Or they can multiply 3 by 10, and subtract 3.

$3 \times 10 = 30$ so $3 \times 9 = 30 - 3 = 27$

Show children how they can use their knowledge of place value to know where to put the decimal point.

3×0.9

$2 \times 0.9 = 1.8$

$3 \times 0.9 = 1.8 + 0.9 = 2.7$

or

$3 \times 1.0 = 3$

$3 \times 0.9 = 3 - 0.3 = 2.7$

additional strategies

partitioning

(see challenges 10, 11 and 13)

Link it

setting out the challenge

getting started

Divide the class into two teams, A and B. On the board, write three multiples of 100 and three single digits. Ask members of each team to carry out the nine multiplications that arise from this set of numbers, and fill in a 3 × 3 OHT grid with the answers, placing them randomly on the grid. Then take the two teams through an abbreviated game of 'Link it'. Each team carries out one of the multiplications and you cover the answer with a counter. The aim is to link three numbers. (For Year 6, replace the multiples of 100 with decimal fractions.)

pairs

The children divide into pairs and choose five multiples of 100 and five single digits. They take a 5 × 5 grid and fill it in with the 25 products found by multiplying their numbers in all their different combinations. They put their answers randomly on the grid.

When the grid is complete, the children exchange grid and numbers with another pair, and then play the 'Link it' challenge. Players take it in turns to choose two numbers (from the two lists), multiply them and cover the answer with a counter. The winner of each round is the first to link four numbers (in any direction).

Play continues for three rounds.

concluding

Ask the children for some of the products (not the numbers multiplied) which were produced as they played 'Link it'. Write these on the board and ask the children what two numbers, of the form they have been working with, might have produced them. Discuss how they work this out.

"How do you know that 900 must have been made by multiplying 300 and 3?"

"How many ways could you get 1200?"

200	2
300	5
700	3

400	900	1000
600	1500	2100
1400	3500	600

Team A

300 x 2 = 600

Team B

700 x 2 = 1400

Team A

300 x 5 = 1500

100	1
300	2
600	4
700	5
900	8

100	300	500	1400	4800
2400	200	400	1800	700
2800	600	3000	600	3500
4500	800	1500	1200	5600
900	2400	3600	7200	1200

round 1

Player One

700 x 2 = 1400

Player Two

300 x 8 = 2400

variations

■ Use two-digit multiples of 10 and single- or two-digit numbers.

30 x 8 or 50 x 37

■ Use decimal fractions.

0·3 x 8 or 0·05 x 7

The deciding factor

unpacking the strategies

mental strategies

doubling one number and halving the other

using closely related facts

using factors

expectations

Year 5: multiply any two-digit multiple of 10 by a single digit, such as 80 × 9

Year 6: multiply any two-digit number by a single digit, such as 58 × 6

Introduce these strategies during the challenge as appropriate.

doubling one number and halving the other

Give children practice in finding factor pairs by applying their knowledge of divisibility. If, for example, they try to divide 96 by 2, they should quickly get 2 and 48.

2 × 48 = 96

Then they can double the 2 and halve the 48 to find another pair.

4 × 24 = 96

By doubling and halving it is possible to explore a range of factors in an even number.

8 × 12 = 96

16 × 6 = 96

32 × 3 = 96

using closely related facts

Show children how they can use facts they know to work out facts they do not know or are unsure of.

4 × ☐ = 96

4 × 20 = 80

4 × 22 = 88

4 × 25 = 100

so 4 × 24 = 96

using factors

Remind children that many numbers are multiples of more than just one number. For example, 12 is a multiple of 3 and 4, and of 6 and 2. These numbers are factors of 12. Remind children of the patterns they can use to identify factors and test divisibility.

Years 5 and 6

If the last digit is 0	you can divide by 10
If the last digit is 0 or 5	you can divide by 5
If the last two digits are 00	you can divide by 100
If the last digit is 0, 2, 4, 6 or 8	you can divide by 2
If the last two digits are divisible by 4	you can divide by 4

Year 6 only

If the total of all the digits is divisible by 3	you can divide by 3
If the number is even and divisible by 3	you can divide by 6
If the total of all the digits is divisible by 9	you can divide by 9
If the last three digits are divisible by 8	you can divide by 8
If the last two digits are 00, 25, 50 or 75	you can divide by 25

additional strategies

using the relationship between multiplication and division   (see challenges 12, 18 and 19)

The deciding factor

setting out the challenge

getting started

Tell the children that you are going to play a guessing game called 'The deciding factor'. Hold up two cards (facing you), each with a mystery number, and tell the children that the product of these two numbers is 96. Ask them to tell you possible options for the two numbers in your hand, and write these on the board. Reveal one card and ask the children to tell you what is on the other card.

target 96

32 and 3

8 and 12

4 and 24

Try another example, with two mystery cards whose product is 40, 64, 39 or 100. Once again consider possible solutions, then reveal one card and invite the children to tell you what is on the other card.

> a game for groups involving factors

groups

Divide the class into groups of three or four. Each group needs a set of twelve factor cards, numbered 1 to 12, and a pile of target cards (taken at random from a pack of 1–100 number cards). Children deal out the factor cards, and look at the numbers they have got. The group then turns over the top target card. Any player who can think of a whole number that, when multiplied by one of their own numbers, gives the target number, tells the group what the multiplication is. If the group agrees, that player scores a point. In some rounds no one will score a point, and in others several players will – or a player may even score more than one point. Used factor cards are returned to the bottom of the pile.

target 100

factor 4

25 x 4 = 100

score a point

> twelve factor cards per group
>
> 1–100 number cards per group

Play continues for five rounds (when the scores are added up and the overall winner declared) or until all the target cards have been revealed.

concluding

Open the discussion up to the whole class to consolidate ideas about multiplication, factors and rules of divisibility.

"How can you find out if a number is divisible by 4?"

"If 4 is a factor of 120, what is its partner?"

variations

■ Include simple fractions.

target 24   mystery cards 48 and $\frac{1}{2}$

■ Children use calculators to check their answers.

■ Add a scoring system, whereby children collect a counter for every factor card successfully used to make a target.

■ Use two mystery cards showing 96 and 8 and announce the target 12. Tell the class that the target is achieved by dividing the larger mystery number by the smaller.

Helter skelter

unpacking the strategies

mental strategies

using place value to multiply and divide by 10, 100 or 1000

using the relationship between multiplication and division

expectations

Year 5: divide multiples of 100 by 10 or 100

Year 6: divide multiples of 100 by 10, 100 or 1000

divide any whole number by 10 or 100

Introduce these strategies during the challenge as appropriate.

using place value to multiply and divide by 10, 100 or 1000

Remind children playing the 'Helter skelter' challenge that, to divide by 10 you move the digits one place to the right, to divide by 100 you move the digits two places to the right, and to divide by 1000 you move the digits three places to the right.

$300 \div 10 = 30$

$300 \div 100 = 3$

$300 \div 1000 = 0 \cdot 3$

Place value boards can help.

	H	T	O	$\frac{1}{10}$	$\frac{1}{100}$
÷ 10	3	0	0		
		3	0		
			3		
			0	3	
			0	0	3

If children seem uncertain of these rules, use a place value chart to practise multiplying and dividing numbers by 10 and 100.

100	200	300	400	500	600	700	800	900
10	20	30	40	50	60	70	80	90
1	2	3	4	5	6	7	8	9
0·1	0·2	0·3	0·4	0·5	0·6	0·7	0·8	0·9
0·01	0·02	0·03	0·04	0·05	0·06	0·07	0·08	0·09
0·001	0·002	0·003	0·004	0·005	0·006	0·007	0·008	0·009

using the relationship between multiplication and division

Give children practice in stating the relationship between two numbers as multiplication and division statements.

4200 was divided by 100 to make 42

42 multiplied by 100 makes 4200

From one such statement, you can make three partner statements.

$42 \times 100 = 4200$

so

$100 \times 42 = 4200$

$4200 \div 100 = 42$

$4200 \div 42 = 100$

additional strategies

partitioning   (see challenges 10, 11 and 13)

using factors   (see challenge 17)

Helter skelter

setting out the challenge

getting started

Write ten multiples of 100 on the board, and invite individuals to read them out.

Play round 1 of a demonstration game of 'Helter skelter' against the class. Choose a number from the board, write it down and cross it off the list – it is now used up. A volunteer from the class does the same.

In the first round, one of you divides your number by 10 and the other by 100; swap over in the second and subsequent rounds, so you take it in turns dividing by 10 and 100. (For Year 6, one divides by 100 and the other by 1000.) Record your answer. Now spin the more/less spinner and read out the result. If it says 'more', the player with the larger number wins a point, and if it says 'less' the player with the smaller number wins a point.

Play another two rounds to decide the overall winner.

pairs

Replace the numbers on the board with new multiples of 100. Invite children to play up to five rounds of 'Helter skelter' in pairs. (You spin the spinner to decide the winner of each round.)

concluding

Note ten of the numbers children created when they divided the numbers on the board by 10 or 100 (or 100 or 1000), and write them, in any order, under the list.

Invite children to match these answers to their multiples in the list above (so, for example, 60 matches 6000). Each time, ask the children to say what the original number was divided by to reach the answer, and what to multiply the answer by to reach the original number. (So, 6000 was divided by 100 to get 60, and you multiply 60 by 100 to get 6000.)

"What is the value of each digit in this number?"

"Can you say the rule for dividing a number by 100?"

variations

- Players divide multiples of 1000 by 100 or 1000; or multiples of 10 by 10 or 100.

- Use numbers with digits other than zero in the tens or ones place, such as 420, 513 or 9630.

- Divide multiples of 10 and 100 by 10, 20, 100 or 200 and aim to get an answer as close as possible to 50 (or 100 or 350…).

3000	4600
500	1200
900	12 300
700	1900
80 700	6300

round 1

Player One (class)

12 300 ÷ 10
1230

Player Two (teacher)

900 ÷ 100
9

spinner: more
Player One: 1 point
class wins round 1

a division
game for pairs

spinner
showing
more/less

400	4200
1500	9900
9000	40 000
7700	2900
10 700	6000

60	420
15	400
99	900
290	77
4	1070

The shrinking machine

unpacking the strategies

mental strategies

using place value to multiply and divide by 10, 100 or 1000

using the relationship between multiplication and division

expectations

Year 5: divide a multiple of 100 by 10 or 100

Year 6: divide any whole number by 10 or 100 giving the answer to one or two decimal places

Introduce these strategies during the challenge as appropriate.

using place value to multiply and divide by 10, 100 or 1000

Remind children that if you can multiply a number by 100, you can also divide a number by 100. To divide by 10 you move the digits one place to the right, and to divide by 100 you move the digits two places to the right.

100	200	300	400	500	600	700	800	900
10	20	30	40	50	60	70	80	90
1	2	3	4	5	6	7	8	9
0·1	0·2	0·3	0·4	0·5	0·6	0·7	0·8	0·9
0·01	0·02	0·03	0·04	0·05	0·06	0·07	0·08	0·09
0·001	0·002	0·003	0·004	0·005	0·006	0·007	0·008	0·009

The place value chart gives children a visual reminder of the fact that numbers greater than 9 (and decimal numbers) are made up of different digits, and that the value of each of those digits is affected by where it sits (its 'place') within the number.

You can also use the chart to remind children of facts about place value. "500 divided by 10 is 50. Divide 50 by 10 and you get 5. Divide that by 10 and you get 0.5…"

Explore with children the effects of different-sized jumps up and down the rows. "If I jump from 2000 to 20 what operation has been carried out? From 30 to 300? 30 000 to 300? 30 000 to 0.3?"

using the relationship between multiplication and division

Make explicit the link between multiplication and division and place value. Use place value boards to show what happens when you multiply and divide numbers by 10 and 100.

	T	H	T	O
			3	4
× 100	3	4	0	0
÷ 10		3	4	0

	H	T	O	$\frac{1}{10}$	$\frac{1}{100}$
		3	4 ·		
÷ 100			0 ·	3	4
× 10			3 ·	4	

When you multiply by 100 and then divide by 100 you end up at the same number.

additional strategies

using factors   (see challenge 17)

The shrinking machine

setting out the challenge

getting started

Invite a child to choose any whole number between 500 and 800 and another child to choose a number (with one decimal place) between 1 and 9. Write the numbers on the board.

705

3·6

Write three possible divisions on the board and ask the children to suggest ways to use one or more of these divisions to get from the first number as close as they can to the second; they may use the same division more than once. Encourage children to use their understanding of place value to suggest divisions beyond those they have been taught.

÷ 10

÷ 100

÷ 2

a division activity for pairs, using decimal notation

Ask the children to help you establish what the difference is between their closest answer and the target, using a calculator if appropriate. (If you use a calculator, encourage the children to predict what the answer will be before checking on it.)

$705 ÷ 100 = 7·05$

$7·05 ÷ 2 = 3·525$

$3·6 - 3·525 = 0·075$

decimal place value chart

pencil and paper

pairs

Children play 'The shrinking machine' in pairs, referring to a place value chart if they need to. Each player chooses two numbers, as before, and uses the three divisions to get from the larger number as close as they can to the smaller one.

round 1

Player One

630

2·5

When they have finished, they exchange only the two original numbers and try using their partner's numbers to get close to the smaller number, again using division. Then the children swap again and check their partner's results against their original workings. Whoever has the smaller difference scores a point.

$630 ÷ 10 = 63$

$63 ÷ 2 = 31·5$

$31·5 ÷ 10 = 3·15$

$3·15 - 2·5 = 0·65$

Children play three rounds of 'The shrinking machine' to decide the winner.

Player Two

800

1·2

concluding

Choose pairs to provide a starting number and target, and then to demonstrate how they got from one to near the other.

"What is the value of each digit in this number: 30·06?"

"How did you decide which of the three numbers to divide by?"

$800 ÷ 100 = 8$

$8 ÷ 2 = 4$

$4 ÷ 2 = 2$

$2 ÷ 2 = 1$

$1·2 - 1 = 0·2$

Player Two wins

variations

- Divide by 2, 3, 5, 10 or 100 (or two or more of these). If necessary, use a calculator in support.

- Choose a starting number and work out the numbers which can be made by dividing it by 2, 10 or 100.

- Choose a target number with two decimal places.

Half and half

unpacking the strategies

mental strategies

using doubling or halving, starting from known number facts

using known number facts and place value

expectations

Year 5: halve any three-digit multiple of 10

double any multiple of 5 to 500

Year 6: double or halve a decimal fraction less than 1 with one or two decimal places

Introduce these strategies during the challenge as appropriate.

using doubling or halving, starting from known number facts

Show children that they can use what they already know to facilitate halving and doubling. If appropriate, identify the parts of a number on a place value chart.

half 630 is half 600 plus half 30

Often children will find it easier to deal with the most significant digit first.

double 285 is double 300 − 15 − 15

and

half 7 is 3·5, which is 3 and 0·5

halve 3 and 0·5 separately to get 1·5 and 0·25

Tell children to jot down intermediate numbers if they think they won't hold them all in their heads.

using known number facts and place value

Point out to children that, with care, halving decimal numbers is no more complicated than halving whole numbers. The difference is that they are dealing with tenths, hundredths and thousandths, instead of tens, hundreds and thousands.

The important thing is to remember to deal with the decimal point.

half 1·8 is ☐

half 18 is 9

18 is ten times bigger than 1·8

so 9 is ten times too big

9 divided by 10 is 0·9

so half 1·8 is 0·9

additional strategies

partitioning	(see challenges 10, 11 and 13)
using closely related facts	(see challenges 10, 16 and 17)
using the relationship between multiplication and division	(see challenges 12, 18 and 19)

Half and half

setting out the challenge

getting started

Write a number on the board.

Tell the children it is the number you reached after you repeatedly
divided a whole number by 2, and that the original number was a
multiple of 100 between 300 and 600 (for Year 6, a number between
1 and 50). Ask them to guess what your starting number was, and
involve the class in testing one or two suggestions.

If no one suggests it, ask them to find what your starting number
might have been by repeated doubling.

pairs

To play the 'Half and half' challenge, each child secretly chooses a
multiple of 100 as a starting number (or for Year 6, a number between
1 and 10) and then halves it repeatedly until they reach the last whole
number (or a number with two decimal places).

They then swap answers – but not starting numbers – with their
partner. The partner must establish what the original number might
be, using repeated doubling.

Go round the class, looking at what children are doing and noting
down any methods you want to emphasise.

concluding

Choose children to explain their methods for halving or doubling
decimal numbers.

"Why do so many of the final numbers have a 5 as the last digit?"

"Can you tell, just by looking at the finishing number, anything about
the starting number?"

Year 5

125

is it 400?

try halving:
200 100

the answer
is not 400

try doubling:
125 x 2 = 250
250 x 2 = 500

the answer is 500

Year 6

4·75

is it 36?

try halving:
18 9 4·5

the answer is not 36

try doubling:
4·75 x 2 = 9·5
9·5 x 2 = 19
19 x 2 = 38

the answer is 19 or 38

Year 5

800 400 200 100 50 25
600 300 150 75

Year 6

6 3 1·5 0·75
4 2 1 0·5 0·25

a halving
activity for
pairs (using
decimal
notation for
Year 6)

pencil and
paper

variations

■ Start with numbers up to 50 or 100.

■ Set a target of 1. Children use two 0–9 dice and a decimal point.
They take turns to roll the dice. They put the decimal point where
they wish. They can then double, halve or stick. The nearest to 1
wins.

roll 3 and 5
0·53
double it
1·06

A cat's whisker

unpacking the strategies

mental strategies

using place value to multiply and divide by 10, 100 or 1000

doubling or halving by dealing with the most significant digits first

expectations

Year 5: multiply a two- or three-digit number by 10 or 100

Year 6: multiply a decimal fraction with one or two decimal places by 10 or 100

Introduce these strategies during the challenge as appropriate.

using place value to multiply and divide by 10, 100 or 1000

Remind children that to multiply by 10 you move the digits one place to the left, and to multiply by 100 you move the digits two places to the left. You may choose to introduce 'A cat's whisker' with a few minutes' practice in multiplying decimal numbers by 10 and 100, using a decimal place value chart.

"0·03 multiplied by 10 is 0·3. Multiply 0·3 by 10 and you get 3. So what is 0·03 multiplied by 100?"

Encourage the children to try different-sized jumps up and down the rows of the place chart, or try experimenting with the abaci, to consider (for example) what happens when you move from 734 to 7·34.

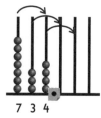

7 3 4

7 ·3 4

doubling or halving by dealing with the most significant digits first

Give children practice in splitting numbers up into their component parts.

double 65·4 is ☐

double 65 and 0·4 which is 130 and 0·8

65·4 × 2 = 130 + 0·8

= 130·8

half 267 is ☐

halve 260 and 7 which is 130 and 3·5

267 ÷ 2 = 130 + 3·5

= 133·5

additional strategies

partitioning   **(see challenges 11, 12 and 13)**

using doubling or halving, starting from known number facts   **(see challenges 15, 20 and 23)**

A cat's whisker

setting out the challenge

calculations
multiplying a two-digit number by 10 or 100

multiplying a decimal fraction by 10 or 100

a multiplication and division game for the whole class

operations dice showing ×10, ×2, ×100, ÷2, ÷10

getting started

Write on the board a number below 10 with one or two decimal places. (For Year 5, write a two-digit number.)

6.54

Also write up these operations.

x10   x100
x2   ÷2

Now ask the children to suggest ways to use one or more of these operations, or the same operation more than once, to get from the first number as close as they can to 100 (for Year 5, 1000). Experiment with their suggestions, reminding children, if necessary, about the effect of multiplying by 10 and 100.

$6.54 \times 10 = 65.4$

$65.4 \times 2 = 130.8$

Invite the class to help you establish the difference between their closest answer and the target of 100 (or 1000).

$130.8 - 100 = 30.8$

individuals

Each child writes down two decimal numbers less than 10. (For Year 5, use two two-digit whole numbers.) You roll the operations dice. (The first roll will have to be a multiplication!) For each roll, the children choose which of their numbers they are going to carry out the operation on.

Continue playing until someone has got both their numbers as close as they can to 100 (or 1000). The winner is the child with the smallest difference (when both the differences are added together).

Year 5

46

$46 \times 10 = 460$
$460 \div 2 = 230$
$230 \times 10 = 2300$
$2300 \div 2 = 1150$
$1150 - 1000 = 150$

Year 6

4.2

$4.2 \times 100 = 420$
$420 \div 2 = 210$
$210 \div 2 = 105$
$105 - 100 = 5$

concluding

Choose children whose work you want to show the class; invite them to demonstrate how they got from their starting number near to 100 (or 1000). As before, invite the class to help you establish the difference between their answer and 100 (or 1000).

"What is the rule for multiplying by 100?"

"When working on 7.91, how did you decide which operation to do first?"

variations

- Start with similar numbers and multiply or divide by 2, 3, 5, 10 or 100 – or two or more of these — to get even closer to 100.

- Start with similar numbers and multiply or divide by 2, 10, 100 or 1000 – or two or more of these — to get close to 5000.

- Choose a decimal number; work out all the numbers that can be made by multiplying that number by 2, 10 or 100, or combinations of these.

Table manners

unpacking the strategies

mental strategies

using doubling or halving, starting from known number facts

expectations

Year 5: double any whole number from 1 to 100

Year 6: multiply any two-digit number by a single digit

Introduce these strategies during the challenge as appropriate.

using doubling or halving, starting from known number facts

Show children how facts in the 16 times table can be derived by doubling – even if they are unsure of the 8 times table.

$6 \times 16 = \square$

Start with a fact you do know, such as 6×2, and keep doubling.

$6 \times 2 = 12$

$6 \times 4 = 24$

$6 \times 8 = 48$

$6 \times 16 = 96$

Tell children that the same strategy, of doubling, can be applied to finding facts in the 24 times table. Children should know their 6 times table by now, in which case they can simply double the numbers in that.

$7 \times 24 = \square$

$7 \times 6 = 42$

$7 \times 12 = 84$

$7 \times 24 = 168$

If they are still unsure of the 6 times table, they can start with the 3 times table.

$7 \times 24 = \square$

$7 \times 3 = 21$

$7 \times 6 = 42$

and so on

additional strategies

using the relationship between multplication and division

(see challenges 12, 18 and 19)

using factors

(see challenge 17)

Table manners

setting out the challenge

calculations
multiplying any
two-digit number
by any single digit

getting started

On the OHP put a 10 × 5 grid with the numbers 1 to 10 across the top and the numbers 2, 6, 8, 12, 16 down the side. (For Year 6, use a 10 × 6 grid and either add a row 24 at the bottom or use a new set of numbers down the side: 12, 15, 16, 24, 25, 31.)

Practise finding some of the numbers that belong in this matrix: point to a cell and ask the children to find the product of its column number and row number – but don't write anything on the grid itself.

teams

Divide the class into two teams. Each team selects someone to choose a cell. Put a counter of their colour on the appropriate square and invite a member of the team to find the product of those numbers. Either check this with an OHP calculator or ask a child to do this. If the child was right, they may keep the counter there – or the team can choose to move it to another cell with the same product. For example, the counter is placed on column 5 row 12: the children agree the product is 60, but decide to move their counter to the intersection of column 10 and row 6.

Continue like this, taking turns for each team. The first team to get three counters in a line, vertically, horizontally or diagonally, wins the game.

concluding

When the game is over, ask the children to help you write in the products on each square of the grid. As you do so, discuss the number patterns and acknowledge the methods children use for calculating the products.

"Look at the pattern of the final digits in this row. How can this help you?"

"We've done 12 times 6, so what will 24 times 6 be? How do you double 72 in your head?"

variations

■ Use different numbers along the top and down the side of the grid, to practise other calculations.

■ Children play this game in twos or threes. The player who is waiting for their turn uses the calculator to check the current player's calculation.

a game for two teams

OHP

transparent counters in two colours

Year 5
OHT 10 × 5 grid

Year 6
OHT 10 × 6 grid

Team A

8 × 7 = 56

Team B

12 × 7 = 84

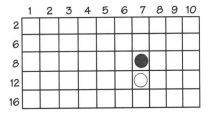

Team A

8 × 6 = 48

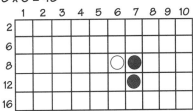

play continues

Squaring up

unpacking the strategies

mental strategies

using known number facts and place value

adding or subtracting a near multiple of 10, and adjusting

using doubling or halving, starting from known number facts

expectations

Year 5: find squares of numbers to 10 × 10

Year 6: find squares of multiples of 10 to 100

Introduce these strategies during the challenge as appropriate.

using known number facts and place value

Tell children that if they use their understanding of place value for these calculations the multiplications become easier.

50 × 50 is the same as (5 × 10) × (5 × 10) = 5 × 5 × 10 × 10

= 25 × 100

= 2500

Discourage the idea of 'adding noughts' when multiplying by 10 or 100 and describe the process as 'moving the digits to the left'.

adding or subtracting a near multiple of 10, and adjusting

Remind children of the strategy for adding multiples and adjusting. Explain that, when a number is either just above or just below a multiple of 10 or 100, the most efficient way to do the calculation is to work with the nearest multiple, do the addition (or subtraction) and then adjust the answer.

7400 + 900 = ☐

= 7400 + 1000 – 100

= 8400 – 100

= 8300

using doubling or halving, starting from known number facts

Look at the diagonal of square numbers on a multiplication grid and discuss which of these numbers appear just once on the grid, such as 49 and 81. These square numbers children will have to remember. Others can be derived using doubling. If you know 2 × 8, you can work out 4 × 8 and then 8 × 8 by doubling.

additional strategies

using closely related facts   (see challenges 10, 16 and 17)

Squaring up
setting out the challenge

getting started

Revise the multiplication of pairs of two-digit multiples of 10. Talk about the strategies for carrying out and checking the calculations.

40 × 30

60 × 90

Write on the board the multiples of 10 up to, and including, 100. (For Year 5, use the numbers 1 to 10.) Ask pairs of children to write these on their blank cards. Now, as a class, work out the square of each number.

...

30	90
40	1600
50	2500

...

a game for
pairs using
squares

blank cards or
slips of paper

Introduce the 'Squaring up' challenge, playing with a volunteer or the whole class, and explain that the challenge involves working together to achieve a final number within the target range. Write up the target range 5000 to 10 000, and the starting number, 1000. (For Year 5, use a target range of 50 to 500 and 100 for the starting number.)

target 5000 to 10 000

start at 1000

Shuffle one set of cards and place them in a pile, face down. Turn over a card and square the number on it. Agree whether to add this square to, or subtract it from, the starting number. Totals may not go below zero.

Repeat this with three other cards, keeping track of the running total on the board. After four cards have been used, if the final total is within the target range, you have won; if not, you've lost.

			total
			1000
40 →	1600	add	2600
80 →	6400	add	9000
60 →	3600	subtract	5400
20 →	400	add	5800

pairs

Children play 'Squaring up' in pairs, recording the numbers they pick, their squares and the running total.

concluding

Prompt children to talk about the mental processes they used, drawing out any generalisations that can be made, and discuss any game strategies they developed.

"When you find the square of 50, how do you know the number of zeros it should have?"

"If you were on 5000 and you picked the card showing 60, what would you do, and why?"

variations

■ Change the starting number or the target number. A starting number higher than the target range will encourage subtraction.

■ Children pick three, or five, cards. Or they pick as many cards as they need to get within the range, then stop.

■ Children pick two cards, square the numbers and add them. If they are within a range of 2000 to 5000, the child wins a point. Then the children shuffle the cards and pick another two. They continue until they have scored five points.

This or that?

unpacking the strategies

mental strategies

using known number facts and place value

doubling or halving by dealing with the most significant digits first

expectations

Year 5: find 50%, 25%, 10% of small whole numbers or quantities

Year 6: find any multiple of 10% of a whole number or quantity

Introduce these strategies during the challenge as appropriate.

using known number facts and place value

Point out to children that many of the percentages in 'This or that?' can be worked out by finding the value of 10% and then multiplying.

20% of £72 is ☐

10% is £7.20

so

20% = £7.20 × 2

= £14.40

Make sure children know how to represent pounds and pence correctly. When dealing with numbers, 14·4 is correct, but when dealing with pounds sterling, the amount should be written £14.40.

2·30 should be written 2·3

but £2.30 is correct

doubling or halving by dealing with the most significant digits first

Children may well suggest that some of the percentages in 'This or that?' can be worked out by halving or doubling. If no one points it out, do so yourself.

50% is half of 100%, so 50% of £10 is £5

25 is half 50, so 25% is half of 50%, or a quarter of 100%

so 25% of £12 is a quarter of £12, which is £3

10% of £12 is £1.20

double this twice to find 40%

so 40% of £12 is £4.80

17·5% of £12 is ☐

17·5% is 10% and 5% and 2.5%

10% of £12 is £1.20

5% of £12 is half of 10% which is £0.60

2·5% of £12 is half of 5% which is £0.30

17·5% of £12 is £1.20 and £0.60 and £0.30 which is £2.10

additional strategies

partitioning

(see challenges 10, 11 and 13)

This or that?

setting out the challenge

getting started

Write a series of percentages on the board. Invite one of the children to select a percentage and then choose from a handful of cards showing different amounts of money (£3, £5, £10, £12, £20, £25, £34, £60, £72, £100). Ask the child to work out how much money they will get.

Repeat this several times with different children.

Now ask individual children to name two percentages and then to choose two money cards. Match percentages with amounts and ask the child to say which they would rather have.

10%	40%
20%	50%
25%	60%
30%	

25% of £60 is £15

50% of £34 is £17

a percentage
activity for
individuals
and groups

one set of
money cards
per group

percentage
spinner
per group

groups

Divide the children into groups of three or four and give each group a percentage spinner and a set of money cards. The children take it in turns for one child to control the spinner and to distribute the money cards, while the other two (or three) children work out, as a group, what the individual percentages are and which amount they would rather have.

Play continues until each group has had four or five turns. Then the group adds up the total money it now has. The group with the most money at the end wins.

concluding

Invite each group to ask another group about one of its pairs of choices, for the rest of the class to hear. Review the methods used to work out the percentages.

"How many steps does it take you to work out what 40% of £100 is? and of £12?"

"How would you work out 75% of £60?"

Group A
(four players)

Player One

distributes the cards
spins the spinner three times

Player Two

£25 →

20%   £5

Player Three

£20 →

40%   £8

Player Four

£10 →

60%   £6

group chooses 40% of £20
which is £8

Player Two

distributes the cards
spins the spinner three times

play continues

variations

■ Children invent their own 'would you rathers?' for a partner to work out.

■ Use gold doubloons instead of sterling, so that children are, in effect, working with numbers rather than money.

■ Find percentages, in the same way, of lengths: of gold chain, or liquorice laces, or some other material children might like.

25% of 120 cm or 50% of 1·3 m

Mental strategies
the full set

Use photocopies of this chart to assess progress.

class assessment

You can use the chart to record your observations and assessments while the session is in progress. Most of the challenges in this book involve children working for a while as individuals, or in pairs or small groups. This can give you an opportunity to note which strategies are being used, and which are not, for follow-up at the end of the session.

Highlight on a copy of the chart those strategies which you expect children to use, or which you have talked about in the first part of the session. Then walk around the class, or spend a while observing a table or group, and tick those which are actually being used. There is room at the bottom of the page to note down anything you may want to follow up – such as methods invented by the children themselves, or particular strategies that need further teaching. Use these notes to provide a focus for the wind-up to the session, or to help you plan future lessons.

individual and group assessment

You may also want to get a clearer picture of how individuals are working – to provide a baseline for comparison purposes in the future; to have a snapshot of their achievements at that particular time; to check whether they are working at full capacity; or to address concerns about any weak areas.

You can use the chart to assess up to six children over the space of a week or more. Write each child's name at the top of a column, and then use the middle part of the lesson to observe them, noting down those strategies which you see them using. Decide beforehand on a recording system that will be most helpful. For example, will you put a tick every time you see a child using a particular strategy? Will you identify those strategies that children appear to have difficulties with? How? Do you need to note the date every time you observe them, or will a more general statement, such as 'month/year', suffice?

a cumulative record

Some schools have a clearly defined strategy for observing the full range of children's potential, and keep detailed records, over time, of each child's achievement in specific key objectives. You can use the chart as a supplement to whatever recording sheet is used for numeracy as a whole – furnishing you with a list of the mental strategies in number calculation that children have demonstrated a knowledge of and prowess in.

a track record

strategies

strategy							
finding a small difference by counting up							
finding a difference by counting up through the next multiple of 10, 100 or 1000							
partitioning into hundreds, tens and ones							
partitioning into thousands, hundreds and tens							
identifying near doubles							
adding or subtracting a near multiple of 10, and adjusting							
adding or subtracting a near multiple of 100 (or 1000), and adjusting							
using the relationship between addition and subtraction							
looking for pairs that make 10 or a multiple of 10							
putting the larger number first							
using known number facts and place value							
using the relationship between multiplication and addition							
subtracting a near multiple of 10, 100 or 1000, and adjusting							
using partitioning to add or subtract pairs of decimal numbers							
using doubling or halving, starting from known number facts							
doubling or halving by dealing with the most significant digits first							
doubling one number and halving the other							
multiplying by 50 by multiplying by 100 and then halving							
multiplying by 25 by multiplying by 100, halving and then halving again							
multiplying by 15 by multiplying by 10, halving and then adding the two answers							
finding sixths, twelfths and twentieths by halving							
using factors							
using closely related facts							
partitioning							
using the relationship between multiplication and division							
using place value to multiply and divide by 10, 100 or 1000							

further reading

Teaching Number Sense
Julia Anghileri
Continuum 2001
a readable account of ways to help
children develop effective strategies
for calculating

The Numeracy File
Mike Askew and Sheila Ebbutt
BEAM Education 2000
articles on teaching primary
mathematics – including mental
strategies – with an emphasis
on innovative and effective
classroom practice

Issues in teaching numeracy
in primary schools
ed. Ian Thompson
Open University Press 1999
essays by leading thinkers in
primary mathematics education,
including a practical emphasis

Teaching primary maths
Mike Askew
Hodder & Stoughton 1998
activities, resources and case
studies that make the link between
the practical and the mental

Talking points
in mathematics
Anita Straker
Cambridge University Press 1993
ideas that encourage children to
use mental strategies

Teaching mental strategies
• number calculations
  in Years 1 and 2
Carole Skinner, Sheila Ebbutt
and Fran Mosley
• number calculations
  in Years 3 and 4
Fran Mosley, Sheila Ebbutt and
Mike Askew
BEAM Education 2001
the first two books in the series

BEAM Education

BEAM Education is a specialist mathematics education publisher.
As well as offering practical support for planning and teaching
mathematics – from Nursery and Reception through to Key Stage 3 –
BEAM actively contributes to research into how children learn
mathematics and how best to teach it.

All BEAM materials are produced in close collaboration with
mathematics specialists and teachers, and offer help with many
of the current classroom concerns voiced by mathematics teachers.
The materials are designed for use alongside other published
schemes, to reinforce learning and stimulate discussion.

BEAM is dedicated to promoting the teaching and learning
of mathematics as interesting, challenging and enjoyable.

BEAM services and materials include:

■ courses and in-school training for teachers

■ consultancy in mathematics education for government
  and other agencies

■ a comprehensive range of teaching accessories

■ over 70 publications for teachers of mathematics.